LIFE'S TOO SHORT!

Pull the Plug on Self-Defeating Behavior
and Turn on the Power of Self-Esteem

Abraham J. Twerski, M.D.

ST. MARTIN'S GRIFFIN ❦ NEW YORK

Design by Sara Stemen

ISBN 0-312-15570-0

10 9 8 7 6 5 4 3

Books are available in quantity for promotional or premium use. Write to Director of Special Sales, St. Martin's Press, 175 Fifth Avenue, New York, N.Y. 10010, for information on discounts and terms, or call toll-free (800) 221-7945. In New York, call (212) 674-5151 (ext. 645).

LIFE'S
TOO
SHORT!

Also by Abraham J. Twerski, M.D.

The Thin You Within You
When Do the Good Things Start?
Waking Up Just in Time
I'd Like to Call for Help, But I Don't Know the Number
I Didn't Ask to Be in This Family
Seek Sobriety, Find Serenity

CONTENTS

INTRODUCTION

In 1965 I became director of psychiatry of a major psychiatric hospital, which served as the primary emergency receiving center for a population of three million and as the admitting service for two major state hospitals, in addition to having a population of three hundred psychiatric patients of its own. The barrage of calls and demands on my energies, both during the day and throughout the night, finally exceeded my saturation point. I had to get away.

In making vacation plans, I sought only one thing: peace and silence. I did not want to go sight-seeing or to be entertained at Disneyland. All I wanted was to be beyond the reach of a telephone and to be left alone.

When someone suggested Hot Springs, Arkansas, this seemed to fit the bill. During the off-season (Hot Springs is a horse-racing town), the community is very quiet. Furthermore, the hot mineral baths might provide relief for my chronic backache.

I checked into a hotel, and the following morning I entered the spa, where I was led into a small cubicle and immersed in a whirlpool bath. This was paradise! Not only was I comforted by the warm, swirling waters, but I was also beyond anyone's reach. The emergency room, social workers, police, nurses, doctors, lawyers, and patients and their families could not reach me. I just relaxed in what was heaven on earth. After six or seven minutes, I emerged from the bath and remarked to the attendant how wonderful this experience had been—just what I needed. The attendant politely told me that I had to return to the bath; the treatment began with soaking twenty-five minutes in the mineral water. I got back in the water, but after five more minutes I again emerged and told the attendant that it was enough. He instructed me that if I did not stay for the full twenty-five minutes I could not continue with the next phase of the treatment. What had begun as heaven was now purgatory. I watched the second hand on the clock move slowly. Each minute seemed an hour, and the final ten minutes of the bath were an eternity, barely tolerable.

Later that day I reflected on what had been a rude awakening. I had been able to take *three years* of a harassing schedule in stride but could not take paradise for more than *seven minutes!*

A bit of analysis led me to conclude that many people are probably not capable of enjoying true relaxation. We are quite adept at enjoying diversion, such as watching television, going to a ball game, reading a book, doing handwork, or chasing a golf ball. All such activities are diversionary because they divert our attention and focus it on whatever we happen to be doing.

What had happened to me in that cubicle was that I had

been deprived of all diversions. There was no one to talk to, nothing to look at, nothing to read, and nothing to listen to. I had been left alone, in the immediate company of myself. All there was in that cubicle was me. I was alone with me. I concluded that my intolerance of relaxation came from my being unable to stand my own company. *I didn't like myself.*

At the ripe old age of thirty-eight, having been a practicing psychiatrist for five years, I began to question why I did not like myself. Eventually I discovered that my image of myself was incorrect. My self-image was quite unlikable. I felt I was a phony. My rabbinical beard and garb portrayed a spiritual person, but I felt I did not measure up to spirituality. I was greedy, envious, selfish, and resentful. I acted as though I were humble, when in fact I was proud and vain. My humility was but a facade for my arrogance. I pretended to be erudite, but my ignorance was overwhelming. I could successfully relate to people only as long as I managed to maintain this facade, but I was always apprehensive that some astute person would see through it to the "real me."

Had anyone told me that I did not know my real self, I would have disputed it. Who else could know me as well as I did? But after a fair amount of self-searching with a bit of help, I discovered that this was indeed the case.

Since then I have been engaged in getting to know myself better, and it has been most rewarding. As you will see, people who have a negative self-image are apt to do many things that are counterproductive, and I was no exception.

I was a "people pleaser," constantly doing things for

others, because I desperately wanted everyone to like me. I felt I had to buy friendship and affection. I never refused a request, regardless of how unreasonable it was, because I could not risk offending or alienating anyone. I pretended I was glad to do the favor, but inside I resented people for imposing on me.

On many occasions I was grossly underpaid for my services, but I acted overjoyed and enthusiastically thanked people for what they had given me. On the other hand, on several occasions when people gave me larger amounts of money in appreciation of something I had done, I refused to accept the bonus in order to impress them.

When others received honors that I felt I deserved, I was magnanimous, pretending to be happy for the recipient of the award, whereas inside I seethed with rage. These were only some of the mechanisms I used to persuade others that I was not the person I felt myself to be.

I feel much different about myself now. When someone asks me to do something, I am free to refuse if I feel it is an unrealistic imposition, and when I do things for others, it is with sincere goodwill. I charge what I feel is a fair fee for my services and do not have to fear that people will accuse me of avarice.

I have proof that my efforts at self-awareness have been successful. I have returned to Hot Springs several times since, and I can fully enjoy twenty-five minutes of relaxation in the whirlpool!

If we have a negative self-image, we may interpret many things as if they are related to us, whereas in reality they have nothing to do with us.

Peanuts® by Charles M. Schulz. Reprinted by permission of United Feature Syndicate, Inc.

The bird sat on Charlie Brown's shoe for a moment, then flew off as birds do. The bird's flight has no connection at all to Charlie Brown, but given that Charlie feels he is unlikable, he interprets the departure as a rejection.

This negative attitude tends to drain people of their energies and may result in self-defeating behavior. In the pages ahead, I investigate this phenomenon and suggest some ways it can be overcome.

But first, why the cartoons? There is truth in the adage that one picture is worth a thousand words. Not only does an illustration convey a message, but it can do so more emphatically. In the cartoon, we can actually feel Charlie Brown's distress and loneliness.

We can see ourselves in a cartoon and identify with the

characters, whereas we might not apply the written word to ourselves. There is often an inherent resistance to recognizing certain behavioral traits in ourselves, and a cartoon may be a vehicle that can help us bypass or break through this resistance.

I have found cartoons to be a potent vehicle in psychotherapy, and I have utilized the brilliant intuitive insights of Charles Schulz in my three books, *When Do the Good Things Start?*, *Waking Up Just in Time*, and *I Didn't Ask to Be in This Family*.

This is a self-help book, and the cartoons are included for their educational value, but there is certainly no harm if they elicit a chuckle. In fact, if we can laugh at ourselves a bit, this is a major achievement. Overcoming self-destructive behavior is important business, but we may be able to handle the challenge better if we stop taking ourselves too seriously.

Part I

Defeating the Self-Image Delusion

ONE

You're Better Than You Think

A young woman was admitted for treatment because of her heroin addiction. All her veins had become obstructed from injecting herself with narcotics, which resulted in multiple abscesses. This otherwise attractive woman was a pathetic sight because of the many lesions.

In the admission interview she told me that she was a nurse and had easy access to drugs. She had used sedatives for insomnia and Percocet for menstrual cramps. These were taken on her own, not prescribed by a physician. She became addicted to both medications, and when she feared that the hospital would note that drugs were missing, she began using street drugs, eventually gravitating toward heroin. The narcotic habit resulted in her being unable to work, and after using up all her savings, she sold everything, including herself, for money to buy drugs.

I noted that she was wearing a locket, which she said was gold, and asked her why she had not sold it for heroin. She said that it was her mother's and that she would never part with it. I asked her to show it to me. After she handed it to me, I picked up a sharp instrument and acted as if I were about to scratch the locket.

"What are you doing?" she asked with a tone of panic.

"Just scratching this a little bit," I said.

"Why do you want to do that?"

"Oh, it's just something I like to do."

"But that's mine!"

"I know. I will give it back to you."

"But I don't want it all scratched up. It's beautiful, and it's valuable to me."

"You mean that when something has beauty and value, you do not allow it to be marred and ruined?" I asked. Then, taking her hands and showing her the bruises and abscesses, I said, "Do you see what this says? These self-inflicted wounds are a loud statement that says 'I am not beautiful. I have no value.' "

People who do not have a sense of self-worth are prone to do destructive things to themselves or inadvertently allow themselves to be injured. Overcoming self-defeating behavior requires self-esteem.

Drug and alcohol abuse are only two of many ways to be self-destructive. The ways we may injure ourselves are legion: dropping out of school, having an unplanned pregnancy, allowing our weight to get out of control, and entering unhealthy relationships are just a few. Most of us are not totally unaware of the destructive nature of our behavior. If we do things that are injurious to ourselves, it is most often not due to ignorance but to an attitude of "I don't really care. It doesn't make that much difference." Even if we protest that we *do* care, on a subconscious level we really do not.

Protecting something valuable is a natural reaction. When we are dressed in fine clothes, we take much more care to avoid soiling them than if we are casually dressed. The proud owner of a new automobile will wash and wax it and avoid pulling up against hedges that might scratch the glossy surface. When we neglect ourselves, it is not that we have lost this natural reaction. As the young woman's concern for the gold locket indicates, she did not consider herself to be of much value or of any beauty.

For more than twenty years, my psychiatric practice has been devoted primarily to problems of substance abuse. I have never encountered a patient who did not have a negative self-image *prior to the use of alcohol or drugs.* Although the consequences of addiction certainly intensify low self-esteem, unwarranted feelings of shame precede the substance abuse in every case.

Many of the examples I cite are cases of alcohol or drug addiction, since these are the ones I see most frequently. But the self-image problem that prevails in this condition is equally present in other self-destructive behavior. Furthermore, just as alcohol or drug addiction is nondiscriminating—it affects both men and women, young and old, rich and poor, learned or illiterate—so are many other varieties of self-destructive behavior. Without exception, the feelings of shame that characterize people with alcohol and drug addictions are a result of a distorted self-perception.

The man in the cartoon on the next page is fortunate; he is aware that the image he sees is a distortion. Think of how someone would feel if he looked into the trick mirror and believed the distorted image to be a replica.

Many problems that bring a person to a psychotherapist's office are the result of this kind of self-devaluation. Sustained recovery from any self-destructive lifestyle requires a change of attitude, one that promotes a positive rather than a negative self-image.

"THANK GOODNESS THIS IS A TRICK MIRROR!"

Learning the truth about oneself and uncovering the beautiful self that exists underneath unhealthful behavior can eliminate shame and a negative self-concept.

Life is too short not to live it as the real you. Putting up a facade is a waste of energy that can leave you drained. Discovery of the "real you" eliminates any necessity for masquerading. It is never too late to make this discovery and live a happier and more constructive life.

TWO

Why You Feel So Bad When You Should Feel Good

Many people may say, "I don't have a distorted self-image. I know myself thoroughly and accurately, and I know for a fact that I am inadequate."

Very capable and gifted people who have come to think of themselves as inadequate may not budge from their belief even in the face of undeniable evidence to the contrary. One woman, a highly skilled physician who had graduated from college summa cum laude and had won the coveted Phi Beta Kappa Award for scholastic excellence, had intense feelings of inadequacy. When I pointed out to her that she could not possibly deny her intellectual superiority, her response was "When they told me I had won the Phi Beta Kappa Award, I knew they had made a mistake."

Again and again I encounter highly accomplished people with profound feelings of inferiority who harbor a negative self-concept.

Where does this negative attitude toward oneself come from, and why is it so prevalent? We might assume that children who grew up under conditions of poverty and emotional deprivation or abuse would develop negative self-concepts. This is often the case. But we find the same feelings of inadequacy and inferiority in people who grew up in stable and comfortable environments with apparently loving and caring parents.

We can only hypothesize why this occurs. A child's only support are his parents, who care for him and serve as a bridge between his needs and his world. The noted psychiatrist Silvano Arieti says that the child must preserve his trust in his parents at all costs. If he sees them as unreliable, the anxiety of being adrift in the world without adequate support is virtually incompatible with sanity. The child must therefore see his parents or other adult caregivers as wise, just, and trustworthy.

Rose Is Rose® by Pat Brady. Reprinted by permission of United Feature Syndicate, Inc.

If parents punish a child, and the child does not fully understand why he is being punished, the child cannot afford to think, "My parents don't know what they are doing." This thought is too threatening. The child instead concludes, "My parents are right. I deserve this punishment because *I am bad*." If the child cannot attribute the punishment to anything he did to warrant it, he concludes, "I am bad. Even if I don't do things that are wrong, I am just bad." The child may develop feelings of shame, guilt, and inferiority, even though he may not have any idea why he should feel this way.

"Life's so unfair! I got spanked first thing when I was born, and I hadn't done anything bad yet!"

Beattie Blvd.™ by Bruce Beattie. Reprinted by permission of Newspaper Enterprise Association, Inc.

Similarly, when things happen that really are irrational, the child may not conclude, "The world is crazy," but rather, "I do not have the capacity to understand," and come to have no confidence in his ability to understand or to make judgments. When feelings like this develop early in life, they may haunt a person well into adult life.

Sometimes a sibling who is younger or has special needs may receive extra attention from the parents. A child may not be able to understand the situation and may conclude: "My parents like my brother/sister more than me. I am not likable."

Various circumstances prevalent in today's society may aggravate the feelings of inadequacy. Years ago, people grew up and lived in the town where their parents and grandparents lived, sometimes even in the same house. Today, multiple generations living in the same community are a rarity. It is interesting to see the trend toward finding one's roots, which seems to indicate that having identifiable and respectable roots gives a person a positive feeling.

Eek & Meek® by Howie Schneider. Reprinted by permission of Newspaper Enterprise Association, Inc.

Roots that are as impersonal as the big bang theory do not contribute much to one's self-esteem.

Also, in today's mobile society, many children attend schools in several different communities before they enter high school, as a result of their parents' changing jobs. Being an outsider and having to work one's way into the existing clique is an ordeal. When this challenge must be repeated several times in a young person's life, it may have a significant impact on his self-concept.

Once a child develops a negative self-image, he is likely to act on that assumption and reinforce his condition. For example, thinking that he is inadequate, he will not try to achieve, because he believes he will fail. Many children do poorly in mathematics because they approach the subject with a preconviction that they are "too dumb" for math. They indeed fail as a result of not trying, and their poor grades confirm that they are "dumb."

These self-fulfilling prophecies may influence many aspects of our behavior, so that by the time we are adults the conviction of inadequacy has been reinforced many times over. A person who develops feelings of inferiority is likely to feel inferior about feeling inferior, and this can develop into a very severe vicious cycle.

"This inferiority complex I've got . . . I assume it's not a very good one, is it?"

Cartoon by Bill Hoest. Copyright Wm. Hoest Enterprises, Inc. Reprinted with permission.

There are many things that people assume to be true that are not at all accurate. Indeed, people who have delusions of inferiority are more convinced of their beliefs than are people who have a correct perception. If a paranoid person believes that the FBI is spying on and persecuting him, no amount of logical argument will dissuade him. His psychotic convictions are as unyielding as the Rock of Gibraltar. A conviction about oneself may contradict the facts, but the person who has come to think of himself as inferior is as unimpressed by facts as is the psychotic paranoid.

Failure to recognize one's personality strengths is somewhat similar to being ignorant of one's assets. Imagine that you are heir to a fortune but do not learn of the bequest. You may be struggling for subsistence when you could be living in luxury.

Everyone encounters difficulties in life. But the person who is out of touch with the reality of his character assets may not be able to utilize these abilities and adjust satisfactorily to the situation.

A patient assumed his position on the psychiatrist's couch, and the doctor said, "Tell me what your problem is."

The patient began, "I have a sixty-four-room mansion located on four hundred acres of beautiful countryside. I have a housekeeper, cook, and chauffeur. My children attend the finest schools. I own three luxury automobiles—"

At this point the doctor interrupted. "I asked you to tell me your problem."

The patient responded, "I'm about to get to that. You see, I make only $150 a week."

Just as a person who has delusions of great wealth runs

into trouble by spending lavishly, so does a person who is intellectually gifted but fails to use these skills.

But what if a person *is* inadequate? After all, some people actually are deficient in various desirable traits. In these cases there is no distortion of the self-perception. But these people usually make a relatively satisfactory adjustment to the reality of their lives. They are not likely to have the various self-destructive behaviors that characterize people with *unwarranted* feelings of shame.

Think of it this way. Suppose you have a small automobile with a four-cylinder engine that is capable of generating sixty horsepower. It doesn't burn up the road, but it gets you where you want to go fairly smoothly. Now suppose you have a car with a powerful V-8 engine that can generate three hundred horsepower, but two of the eight cylinders are not functioning. It still generates more than two hundred horsepower, but it does not give you a smooth ride. Why? Because smooth performance requires all eight cylinders to be functioning.

As with engines, so with people. A person with lesser endowment may make a satisfactory adjustment to his limited capacities, while a person of much greater capacities who thinks he is defective may make a less satisfactory adaptation to life.

Let me cite an incident in my own childhood that illustrates the ability to adjust to inadequacies.

As a child, I was an avid baseball fan. This was not an unusual phenomenon in the era of Lou Gehrig, Joe Di-Maggio, Ted Williams, Bob Feller, and other giants of baseball fame. I had a burning desire to play baseball, but I was hampered by two real problems: I couldn't hit and I couldn't catch. I was clearly a liability on any team, and consequently I was never chosen to play.

Hoping to buy a position on the team, I came to the playground and gave all the kids caramels. They gladly took the candy, but I still was not chosen to play.

In desperation, I resorted to another maneuver. Not far from the playground there was a sporting goods store that displayed a bat in the window. This was no ordinary bat. It was a shiny brown Louisville Slugger with a royal blue felt handle and with Lou Gehrig's signature etched into it. Before and after school the kids would push their noses against the windowpane, trying to get as close a look as possible at the dream bat.

This bat was indeed only a dream. It sold for $1.25 at a time when the average family lived comfortably on $30 a week and when $18.75 could buy a suit with two pairs of pants. No child could think of spending $1.25. However, I saw it as my only hope of getting to play baseball.

I had a bank that held the nickels, dimes, and quarters that I received from members of my father's congregation as Hanukkah favors. I was not supposed to touch this money, but it was a matter of life and death. I pried the bank open, took out $1.25, and purchased the bat.

The kids at the playground were in disbelief. "Lookit! The kid! He's got the bat! Hey, kid, can we use the bat?"

"Only if I play," I said.

The two team captains chose their sides, and after everyone had been chosen, I remained with the coveted bat.

"Well, someone's gotta take him. It's his bat."

"We don't want him. You take him."

"Why should we take him? We got Eddie, and he stinks!"

The bickering went back and forth until one captain came up with a Solomonic solution. "Okay, we take him, but his outs don't count."

After several days, the folly of going through the motions of striking out was evident, and I withdrew from the game, letting the kids use my bat anyway. From then on I spent recess studying.

This was hardly an ego-edifying experience, but I look back on it with amusement. It registers no discomfort whatsoever. Although it was unpleasant at the time, I do not associate any feelings of humiliation with it.

Why? Because the defects involved were real. I couldn't hit or catch a ball. I was not athletic. So what? I had other areas of potential excellence, such as scholastic abilities, and I developed them instead. We can compensate in various ways for an actual limitation. It is only the misperception of fantasized defects that gives rise to psychological problems.

Let us now look at some of the things that happen when people have imaginary defects. They may try to cover up these defects, which often results in awkward behavior. Since these kinds of "cover-ups" are common, we may be able to identify our own use of such techniques by observing them in others. If we can understand that the defects we are trying to conceal are imaginary, we may be able to dispense with these maneuvers and make much more satisfactory adjustments to various life situations.

Part II

Understanding the Problems of Low Self-Esteem

THREE

Fear of Rejection

R alph had accumulated a string of unsuccessful roman-tic relationships. He dated frequently but was never able to develop an ongoing relationship. The young women he met showed some initial interest in him, but without exception they subsequently turned him away. Ralph had resigned himself to this situation.

Ralph's best friend was in the Navy and was given an assignment that would take him out to sea for at least six months. He therefore asked Ralph to take out his girlfriend and show her a good time once in a while. Ralph did so, and she fell in love with him.

What happened is easily explained. Ralph had a very poor self-image. He was convinced that no woman would be interested in him if she saw the "real" Ralph, so he tried to impress his dates by putting on a facade that was artificial and awkward and resulted in the reverse of what he hoped. When he was entertaining his buddy's girlfriend, he was not trying to impress her and was relaxed and natural. This gave her the opportunity to see the *real* Ralph, with whom she fell in love.

Arlo & Janis by Jimmy Johnson. Reprinted by permission of Newspaper Enterprise Association, Inc.

Yes, we often expect people to act "natural" when photographing them, and it seems to escape us that posing is not natural. Ralph's posing in order to impress women was about as natural as Joey posing for his father. Little wonder that his dates found him unattractive. When he stopped his posing, his natural, pleasant personality came through.

The terms *self-image* and *self-perception* convey a concrete idea. If we perceive an object, we assume it is there just as we see it. We do not think, "Perhaps that object is really not there, and I am just hallucinating." When we see an image, we assume it to be real. Our perceptions tell us what reality is, and we act according to our perceptions.

We naturally assume that what we perceive to be reality is also what others perceive as reality. If I see a bus coming down the street, I naturally assume that everyone else sees a bus coming down the street.

This is also true of a self-image or a self-perception. If I see myself in a certain way, that is reality. I do not go around thinking that my perception may be distorted. If my self-image is one of inadequacy and inferiority, then I am certain that other people perceive me as such.

If my self-image is negative, and I am convinced that others see me negatively, this poses a serious problem for me. Why would anyone deserve my companionship? Since it is obvious to me that no one would wish to be in my presence, any effort that I make to associate with people will inevitably result in their rejecting me. Since rejection is extremely painful, I must avoid it at all costs. Clearly the most effective method of avoiding rejection is to avoid associating with people. I become a "loner." I prefer to be by myself.

Most loners say that they prefer to be alone because they are private people and don't like others intruding on their privacy. Do not believe this; they are lying either to you or to themselves. Loners crave companionship as much as everyone else does, but their fear of rejection outweighs their desire for companionship.

Not all people with a negative self-image are loners. Some may think, "Of course, if anyone got to know me, he would reject me. But I am clever enough to put on a facade so that people will not get to know the true me." These people can be very entertaining socially. They feel safe in public because they can act in a way that prevents others from getting to see the "true self."

The telltale feature of this latter type is that they may feel threatened by intimacy. It is one thing to put on an act for a few hours in a superficial relationship where we may feel safe in being able to conceal the "true self." It is another thing to be exposed day after day to the same person in an intimate relationship. "Oh, no! I can't continually put on an act! Sooner or later she will see through the facade and then leave me for sure."

Many couples have a wonderful courtship, but the relationship turns sour soon after marriage. Other couples have a grand time dating, but as soon as there is any talk about commitment, one or both partners terminate the relationship. The reason in both cases is the same: Intimacy may constitute a threat of exposure, and exposure, they feel, is certain to result in rejection. To avoid rejection, avoid intimate relationships.

There is another mechanism that dooms relationships, and that is precipitation of rejection.

Bob was a handsome, personable, straight-A student whose self-image was the opposite of his actual self. He perceived himself as homely, dull, and unintelligent. When he met Carol, a charming student nurse, he thought he didn't stand the slightest chance. He was flabbergasted when she agreed to go out with him. He was even more surprised when she continued to date him.

Bob could not understand why a young woman as lovely as Carol gave him the time of day. He concluded that the reason Carol accepted his requests for dates was that she was very sensitive and did not want to hurt his feelings. He knew that this could not be a lasting relationship. Obviously, Carol was not going to make a long-term commitment out of pity for him. He therefore knew that it was inevitable that she would terminate the relationship. Whenever he picked up the phone to call her, he was overcome with intense anxiety. This is the time she is going to say it. "Bob," she will say, "it's hard for me to say this to you. I don't want to hurt your feelings. You're really a swell person, but I just can't see you anymore." He knew that she was going to say it, just as he knew that the sun was going to rise in the east.

When Carol did not reject him and agreed to go out with him, Bob was overjoyed. But when he called her the next time, the anxiety over the anticipated rejection recurred even more intensely. The suspense over the rejection that he was certain was forthcoming became so unbearable that he sent her father a telegram: "Congratulations. In seven months you'll be a grandfather." Carol told him never to call her again.

Bob tormented himself for having precipitated this rejection, but it is clear why he did so. Painful as it was, the rejection was a finality. Living with the suspense and anticipation of its imminent occurrence was intolerable. Getting the rejection over with was the lesser of two evils.

A variation of this theme occurred with Frank and Lois, who had been happily married for seventeen years. Frank was a building contractor, and they were financially comfortable. When their youngest child began attending school all day, Lois sought something productive to do with her time, and after completing courses received her realtor's license. After she made several sales, Frank underwent a radical personality change. He became irascible, screaming at her when she left the house to show a home to prospective buyers. "A married woman should not be going out alone at night!" "On weekends a mother should be home with her children." Lois did not know what to make of this Jekyll and Hyde transformation and convinced Frank to see a psychiatrist.

The dynamics of this case were easily detected. Frank's self-image was profoundly negative, and he could not believe that Lois truly loved him. He felt that the only bond in their marriage was that he provided her with economic security. If she were to become economically self-sufficient, there would be no reason for her to stay with him. He saw her newly acquired earning capacity as undermining the marriage, and he fought it aggressively, almost succeeding in ruining their marriage with his erratic behavior. Eventually, with counseling, Frank was able to accept that Lois's love for him was genuine.

These are only a few of the ways a negative self-image can lead to self-defeating behavior in relationships.

FOUR

Demanding Recognition

The feeling of being insignificant can be so devastating that some people take radical measures to make certain that their existence is recognized. If we think back to grade school, we can remember the class clown who called attention to himself by overt misbehavior. His being singled out by the teacher and being sent to the principal's office was a desperate attempt to be noticed. Such maneuvers are by no means restricted to young people.

If we feel distressed because of a negative self-image and think that other people do not appreciate us, we may seek recognition in an effort to convince ourselves as well as everyone else that we are respectable people and are not as bad as we are afraid we may be. We may push for recognition in different ways. For example, David always insists that the banquet committee seat him at a conspicuous place just in front of the speakers' table. He doesn't realize that he is forcing himself on others. Even if they cater to his whims, this does not endear him to them. To the contrary, such techniques make him less desirable company, and he may precipitate the very thing he is trying to avoid.

When inviting people to a family celebration, the host may say, "I better get Aunt Vera's invitation out first. If we somehow forget her, or if she thinks anyone else was invited before her, we'll never hear the end of it." Aunt Vera demands recognition "or else," which is hardly likely to elicit much affection.

There is nothing wrong with wishing to be recognized, but when we feel good about ourselves we assume that our presence is noticed at least by some people. If we feel inferior, we may feel that our presence is not noted at all, or if it is, it is not noted adequately by a sufficient number of people.

Following a public lecture, there is often a question-and-answer period. Many people ask pertinent questions of the speaker, but every so often someone delivers a speech. There is little doubt that this person wants to make everyone in the audience aware that he is there and has something to say, even though it may have nothing to do with the subject of the lecture. The folly of such a maneuver is that the inappropriateness of this person's comments may cause people in the audience to feel that he is a fool. This is an example of how some maneuvers to escape the negative self-image feelings backfire. This person, who desperately seeks to impress others, actually causes them to think poorly of him.

Demanding recognition in order to overcome feelings of shame and inferiority is as futile as trying to fill a bottomless pit. Just as the drug addict may require ever-increasing doses of narcotics to get high, the person who seeks recognition is likely to be chronically dissatisfied and constantly demand greater recognition.

"Guess what, Roger! I'm going to be on the 11-o'clock news!"

Cartoon by Bill Hoest. Copyright Wm. Hoest Enterprises, Inc. Reprinted with permission.

These desperate attempts not only are ineffective in bringing about the desired results but destructive; they produce a lowering of self-esteem, which in turn provokes the person to even more radical measures.

FIVE

Co-Dependence

The term *co-dependence* initially came into use in reference to a family member—usually a spouse—of an alcoholic or other chemically dependent person. The addict was the "dependent" person, being literally dependent on a chemical, and the co-dependent was the "significant other," who was often an "enabler," catering to the addict's needs and whims. A typical description of the dependent/co-dependent relationship is that the dependent person plays a tune and the co-dependent answers to it. It is said that the co-dependent sometimes is sicker than the dependent person.

Recently, co-dependency has been applied to relationships other than addiction in which one person plays a tune and the other dances to it; the latter is not doing what he or she really wants to do but what another expects. The "dancers" may lose control of their own lives and destiny because their behavior is being dictated by someone else.

If we have good self-esteem, we are unlikely to be manipulated. Others may try to change our personality,

"I KNOW THERE'S SOMETHING EMOTIONALLY WRONG WITH MY HUSBAND. HE SPENDS HIS ENTIRE DAY AT THE BAR."

but we can stand our own ground. Of course, standing one's own ground may not always be commendable; sometimes a personality could benefit from constructive changes.

But if we lack a firm sense of self, we are vulnerable to allowing others to define who we are. We may take on a chameleon-type existence, being one thing for our spouse, another for our employer, another for our minister, another for friend A, another for friend B, and so on.

"Stop trying to change me."

Cartoon by Bill Hoest. Copyright Wm. Hoest Enterprises, Inc. Reprinted with permission.

Yes, people with "soft tops" are likely to be convertibles.

Willy 'N Ethel by Joe Martin. Reprinted with special permission of North American Syndicate.

Here's a broader definition of co-dependency:

Co-dependency is the denial or repression of the real self. It is based on the wrong belief that love, acceptance, security, success, closeness, and sal-

> vation are *all* dependent upon one's ability to do "the right thing." In the process, the co-dependent denies who [he/she] really is.*

This definition can apply not only to family members of chemically dependent people, but also to the alcoholic or addict. It is an adaptation that is often found in people who grew up with an alcoholic parent or a parent who was dysfunctional in other ways. Since dysfunction of various kinds is widespread, it should come as no surprise that many people have developed co-dependency traits.

Patricia is the second child in a family. Her father had hoped for a boy and grudgingly accepted his fate when the first child was a girl. When Patricia was born, the second disappointment was a bit too much. When Patricia soon discovered that she was supposed to have been a boy, she felt that in order to get her father's love, which she fervently desired, she had to *be* a boy. She developed tomboyish behavior, hoping to satisfy her father. Unfortunately, her best efforts fell short of the mark, because to Patricia's father, a tomboyish girl was still a girl.

When Patricia was eight, the blessed event occurred—a son was born. Still vying for her father's affection, Patricia doted on her brother, hoping to forestall her father's transferring all his love to the real boy in the family. She continued to be the tomboy, especially since Chris was still an infant. When Chris was not quite three, their mother came down with multiple sclerosis, and Patricia, rather than the older sister, took on the obligation of being the mother in the family. Patricia thus played the role of boy, nursemaid

---

*Robert C. Subby, *Lost in the Shuffle* (Deerfield Beach, Calif.: Health Communications, 1987).

to Chris, nurse to her mother, and surrogate wife—all in order to merit the affection and attention of her father. She never gave any thought to what she wanted to be herself.

Patricia's older sister married, Chris joined the Army at eighteen, and then her mother died. Patricia fell in love. The young man was accepted in law school, and it was the natural thing for Patricia to help support him through his training. After all, she was Patricia the caregiver, who cared for people to earn their affection. Her first child was born before Bob completed law school, and it was not too much for her to care for the child and continue to work. She had been well prepared to sacrifice her own needs in order to care for others.

After the second child was born, Patricia began feeling tired. She was often completely drained by the end of the day. Bob was putting in long hours at the office, and Patricia was alone and lonely. She had given to everybody, but no one was giving to her. She had no one, not even herself, because there had never been a "self." She sensed her neediness and felt guilty about it, because she was not supposed to be a needy person. To the contrary, she was supposed to provide for the needs of others, because that is what would make her likable. Having needs of her own would mean making demands on others, and people might become alienated if she wanted them to give to her instead of her giving to them. Besides, who was there that could give to her? Dad was six hundred miles away and had remarried. The children were little and needed care. Bob was hardly ever home. Like an empty bank account, Patricia was emotionally depleted.

At some point Patricia found that taking a drink assuaged her loneliness and alleviated her guilt. Alcohol made life more tolerable.

There is no need to go on with the details of Patricia's story, which developed into a textbook case of alcoholism. She made the circuit of doctors and psychiatrists, becoming addicted to pills, attempting suicide, and ultimately losing Bob and the custody of her two children.

The entire tragic tale can be traced back to a single factor: Patricia had never had a self and had never considered what she really wanted to do with her life. She was a co-dependent, convinced that the only way to be loved was to be of service to others. Her identity was totally dependent on what others thought of her, rather than on what she thought of herself.

Not all co-dependence takes as tragic a course as Patricia's, but the principle in her story can be applied more generally. People who lack an internal identity and fashion themselves according to what they think others want them to be in order to find favor with them invariably make wrong choices, detracting from their self-fulfillment and happiness.

Developing a sense of self does not mean being selfish. There are, of course, times when putting one's own needs first is inconsiderate and selfish, but if we understand what a sense of self and identity is all about, we can see that this is not the kind of selfishness that is morally reprehensible.

When flying in a plane, the flight attendant announces, "In the event of the loss of cabin pressure, oxygen masks will appear before you. If you are traveling with a child, put your own mask on first and then assist the child with his." Can you expect a devoted mother to be so selfish as to put her interests before that of her child? But there is a valid reason for these instructions. Once the mother is receiving oxygen, she can make certain the child gets his, and both will be safe. If she attempts to help the child first, she may become confused due to oxygen deprivation and unable to put the child's mask on properly. Neither she nor the child will get oxygen. *The mother must assure her own well-being in order to help the child.*

This is the principle of developing a sense of self and an identity. Patricia's adaptation to what she thought her father wanted her to be and then being a caregiver ultimately resulted in her two children having an unhappy mother, then an exhausted mother, then an alcoholic mother, and finally no mother at all. The two human beings she had brought into the world and for whom she had prime responsibility did not get proper parenting because of Patricia's desire to be everything to everybody. There is nothing noble or praiseworthy about this kind of self-sacrifice.

There is little that Patricia could have done about herself as a child. Ideally, parents love their children unconditionally and children feel this and are secure in their parents' love for them. But the ideal is not often achieved. Patricia may have been reading her father correctly, and when she was a child, her reaction was completely understandable. If her mother had detected what was happening, she might have been able to help Patricia or avail her of competent counseling. But there were no gross signs of trouble for her mother to identify. Everybody seemed fairly happy, so why assume otherwise?

Although Patricia showed no overt signs of unhappiness until relatively late, there was still time for appropriate therapy. If her early recourse to alcohol had been picked up as an act of desperation and the proper treatment sought, Patricia could have been helped to stop trying to buy love and affection. She could have been helped to a sense of self-esteem, to believe that she was a good person who deserved to be loved and who would be loved even if she did not efface herself in order to provide for others. At this point, Bob could have been brought in as an ally, and he could have helped her realize she was indeed lovable. With proper group support, sharing her feelings and discovering that she was not alone in how she felt about herself, Patricia could have relinquished her desperate efforts to buy the affection that she could really get for free. She could have discovered that she did not have to be the super person she thought she must be, but simply be a good, adequate wife and mother, who deserved to receive and to be cared for just as much as she was expected to give and care for others.

It is never too late to acquire a sense of self. If you recognize that you grew up in a dysfunctional family, be aware that you are at high risk for being co-dependent. You would do well to familiarize yourself with the symptoms of co-dependency. You would also be wise to seek out support groups that are sensitive to these problems, such as Adult Children of Alcoholics, Co-dependents Anonymous, or Families Anonymous. Even if you do not have any disabling symptoms, you might nevertheless consider an evaluation by a competent psychologist, just as you undergo a routine medical checkup even when you feel well.

The conditions that can result in co-dependence are ubiquitous and legion. The misery that co-dependence can cause for you and for others, especially your children, is often avoidable. You don't need to be this way. Life's too short.

SIX

Hypersensitivity

People with a negative self-image may be exquisitely sensitive. Things that do not affect anyone else may elicit a marked reaction. It's much like someone who has a severe sunburn: A light touch causes her to wince with pain. The sunburned person knows that her skin is unusually sensitive and does not impart hostile intent to the person who touched her. But people with a negative self-image may not be aware that they are abnormally sensitive. When someone says or does something that causes them emotional pain, they are likely to conclude that the other person intentionally insulted or provoked them.

A man comes home from work, enters the house, and says, "Hello, everybody. I'm home!" The wife and children are in the den, watching an interesting television program. They respond with "Hi, honey" and "Hi, Daddy." A person with a positive self-image who knows that his wife and children love him will hang up his coat, go into the den, and embrace his family. Someone who is overly sensitive will say, "Hi, honey? Is that the kind of appreciation I get for working all day to feed and clothe my family? The damn television program is more important than coming out to welcome me. What an ungrateful bunch!" From that point on, the evening is apt to go downhill. Little love can be generated in either direction when someone is bristling with resentment.

The wife and children may have been very happy to have the husband and father home. They may fully appreciate his efforts on their behalf. The fact that they did not leave the television set at a high point in the program and run out to greet him is in no way an indication of their lack of love or admiration. However, because he seriously doubts that he deserves being loved, he interprets their failure to greet him as a confirmation of his feelings about himself.

Constructive criticism can result in improving ourselves. Whether it is an instructor who corrects our work or a friend who makes a legitimate observation about something we say or do, we can learn to avoid mistakes and to do things in a better way.

People with a negative self-image, however, may be so sensitive that they react adversely to constructive criticism. Believing that they are inadequate and fearing that others will detect their inadequacies, they may take a critical remark as evidence that their inadequacies have been exposed. They may respond to a critical remark as though it were an insult, and this reaction may be detrimental to others as well as to themselves.

How intensely a negative self-image can affect our response to criticism is demonstrated by a personal experience. Many years ago, while I was still in the throes of my own negative self-image, I was invited to deliver several lectures at a continuing education course for alcoholism and drug counselors. More than one hundred therapists had enrolled for the course, and the month afterward I received a packet with their evaluations of my lectures. As I paged through, my ego soared. Everyone was saying very flattering things about my presentation. Then I came to one review that was very critical. I was devastated! For two weeks I was depressed, until it dawned on me that 109 to 1 is an excellent score. Clearly the 109 favorable evaluations were correct. However, my initial response was to remember that Lincoln had said that you can fool only some of the people. I thought that I had succeeded in fooling 109 of the attendees, but this one person saw through my act and knew the truth about me. Feeling negative about myself resulted in my interpreting a 109 to 1 vote in favor of the single dissenting opinion!

How we feel about ourselves can also determine how we react to criticism and insults. These are never pleasant, but we can react along a spectrum from indifference to violence.

A young woman completed her treatment for alcoholism but returned home to a very difficult marriage. I followed her progress in recovery, and she was doing extremely well. About a year later I received a phone call from her. She was sobbing. Eventually she was able to tell me that she could no longer take her husband's verbal abuse. He constantly accused her of being a failure as a wife and mother.

After she calmed down a bit, I asked her to listen very carefully to what I had to say. "I think that the scar on the right side of your face is repulsive," I said.

After a moment of silence she said, "Pardon me?" I repeated my unkind remark, and she said, "I don't understand."

"What is there not to understand? I spoke plain English."

"But I don't have a scar on my face."

"Then what did you think when I told you how ugly it was?"

"I didn't understand what you were talking about."

"You see," I pointed out, "when I say something derogatory to you and you know it is not true, you don't react with hysterical sobbing. Instead you say, 'I don't know what you are talking about.'

"When your husband insulted you and you knew he was wrong, your reaction should have been 'You must be hallucinating. I am an excellent wife and mother.' You might not have been happy about what he said, but you did not have to react so intensely.

"I suspect that your reaction was due to your thinking that he might be right. Even though it is early in your recovery, you are functioning extremely well. We never deny our dereliction during the active addiction, but that is now a thing of the past and we should be focusing on the positive aspects of recovery. A positive attitude toward yourself would have made your husband's comments merely irritating, not demolishing."

None of us likes being the target of derogatory remarks, but how we react to them may depend to a great extent on how we think of ourselves.

It has been said that no one can put me down except myself. When we feel good about ourselves, uncomplimentary remarks and even frank insults may not exactly roll like water off a duck's back, but they can be much more easily dismissed and certainly need not make us feel worse about ourselves.

SEVEN

Narcissism

L loyd requested a psychiatric consultation. His problem? He had had a relationship with a woman whom he claimed he loved very much but to whom he had been both verbally and physically abusive. She finally terminated the relationship and refused to see him. He now recognizes how wrong he was and deeply regrets his behavior. He will never act this way again. He wants her to know this so that she will consider renewing their relationship, but she won't talk with him. He hoped that I would call her and, as a psychiatrist, tell her that I have determined that he is sincere in his remorse and that she should give him another chance.

I told Lloyd I would do no such thing. He cried, pleading that he be given the chance to prove himself and insisting that this was the most important thing in his life. He continued to call me several times a day, and when I refused to vouch for him, he drove to the woman's home and accosted her as she left for work. She promptly called the police. He then slashed her tires and made threatening phone calls, harassing the woman whom he claimed to "love" so deeply.

Psychologists use the term *narcissism* to describe a person who is extremely self-centered and self-adoring. The term comes from the Greek myth of Narcissus, a handsome young man who fell in love with his own reflection. In reality, narcissists do not love themselves at all. They are indeed self-centered and demand that everyone else adore and respect them, but this is precisely because they do *not* love themselves. Narcissistic people have extremely poor self-images, and they are scared that they cannot be loved or appreciated. They are so terrified that they may forcefully demand to be loved and respected because they doubt that it can happen spontaneously. Narcissism is thus an extreme form of hypersensitivity.

Lloyd is a narcissist. If he genuinely cared for the woman, he would not have harassed her. But Lloyd cared primarily for himself. He perceived her rejection as a blow to his fragile ego. Lloyd's case is typical. The behavior of narcissists is invariably self-defeating, since their need to possess and dominate frightens people away.

Being rejected in a romantic relationship is always unpleasant. But if we have a positive self-image we are likely to react more realistically. After the wound heals, we can conclude, "I guess we were not meant for each other," and go on to develop other relationships. The narcissist, however, has serious doubts about his or her lovability and reacts to rejection as if this were a life-threatening event.

There are other areas of exquisite sensitivity that may

elicit a severe reaction from a narcissist. Lloyd's related to his doubts of lovability. People who have serious doubts about their competence may react somewhat similarly when they feel that their abilities are being questioned.

As another example, let us look at two women who became physicians. A developed a negative self-image early in life, although she is very talented. The discomfort of feeling inadequate caused her to seek ways to escape this distress, and noting that doctors are highly respected, she chose a career in medicine. The M.D. after her name would be prestigious, and the gratitude from patients would help her overcome her feelings of inferiority.

Feelings of inferiority that have no basis in reality cannot be corrected by such maneuvers. If your television set is broken, a repairman can restore it to proper function. If it is not broken, but you just don't happen to like the picture, nothing the repairman can do will satisfy you. Replacing tubes and other parts that are in fact not defective will accomplish nothing.

Some people do have actual defects, for which they can compensate in reality. A person who has lost his vision may develop a very keen sense of touch or hearing, which can help compensate for the absence of sight. But he cannot compensate for a deficit that exists only in his imagination.

A's negative self-image is a delusion. She is oblivious to her many positive assets, and no amount of compensation will eliminate this misconception. Seeing the M.D. after her name may temporarily soothe her, but feelings of inferiority will continue to haunt her. When a grateful patient thanks her for her help, it is like aspirin for a chronic headache, relieving the distress for only a brief period of time. A is in constant need of reassurance.

B, on the other hand, is no more gifted than A, but she grew up with a positive self-concept. She knows she is bright, and she considers herself a likable person. B, too, chose a medical career, but not for A's reasons. B thought she would enjoy the practice of medicine. She wishes to help people and feels good when she does so. But she is not dependent on their gratitude for a sense of well-being.

Let us now take a patient into these two doctors' offices and see how their self-image influences the way they relate to the patient.

John Doe consults Dr. B because of abdominal distress. Dr. B takes a careful history, performs a physical examination, and does several blood tests. On the basis of these, she assures John that there is nothing seriously wrong with him and suggests an appropriate diet to eliminate the abdominal discomfort.

Two weeks later John returns, complaining that the pain has worsened. Dr. B decides to do a complete workup and has John undergo upper and lower gastrointestinal X rays, kidney studies, and a sonogram. After these are completed she shares with John the good news that there is no sign of any tumor, ulcer, gallstones, or kidney stones. The pain, Dr. B explains, is due to a spastic condition of the intestines, which should be relieved by antacids and anti-spasmodic medication, which she prescribes.

Two weeks later John again appears in Dr. B's office, doubled up with pain, complaining that the medication has not helped and that he hasn't slept a single night in the past two weeks.

Dr. B feels bad that she has not been able to help John but does not feel threatened by John's failure to recover. Dr. B knows that she is a competent physician and genuinely wants to help John, so she tells him, "This stumps me, John. I can't put my finger on the reason for your pain. Let me refer you to a gastroenterologist."

Now let's see what happens if John consults Dr. A instead. The first two visits go exactly as they do with Dr. B. However, when John returns for the third visit with a persistent complaint of pain, Dr. A does not respond the way Dr. B does.

Remember, Dr. A needs her patients to tell her how wonderful they feel and what a great doctor she is. John's persistent complaints of pain are a threat to Dr. A's ego, so she interprets these complaints as a reflection on her adequacy, as though John has said, "What kind of doctor are you, anyway, that you are not helping me?" The nagging feelings of inadequacy that have plagued Dr. A since childhood are reinforced by John's failure to improve.

Dr. A is likely to respond in one of three ways:

"Hmm," Dr. A says pensively. "This is more serious than I thought, John. There must be something that is not showing up on the X ray. I believe we should do an exploratory laparotomy to get at the source of the trouble."

There are certainly cases where exploratory surgery is necessary, but this is not one of them. Dr. A hasn't the foggiest notion what she is looking for. She is essentially going on a fishing expedition in John's abdomen, and is doing so because she cannot admit that she doesn't know what the problem is. She cannot refer John to a gastroenterologist because admitting that others may know something she doesn't is an affront to her fragile ego. In order to assuage her own ego pain, she subjects John to surgery.

An alternative response may be:

"Look here, John. The tests we have done are absolutely thorough. There is simply nothing that could be causing your pain. It is psychosomatic pain, all in your head. You need psychiatric help, and I am going to refer you to a psychiatrist."

In this response, Dr. A thinks—mistakenly—that John is accusing her of not being a good doctor. "Well," Dr. A thinks, "I'll tell you something. You're crazy. Your opinion doesn't count for anything. You need your head examined!"

Here is another possible response:

"I'm sorry that the cause of your pain isn't showing up, John. I am going to give you something to help you feel better. Here is a prescription for pain medication, which you take every four hours. I will also give you something to help you sleep at night."

John begins taking the medication as prescribed. But, as is common, several weeks or months later, his body becomes accustomed to the medications and they no longer have an effect. John increases the doses and eventually develops a serious addiction to pain pills and sedatives.

Any of Dr. A's responses are detrimental to John. Dr. A is primarily concerned with protecting her fragile self-image, and all three diagnoses are directed more toward her own needs than John's.

Whether it is doctor-patient, teacher-student, counselor-client, or any type of service delivery, results are likely to be unfavorable when the person delivering the service is motivated more by his or her own needs than by those of the recipient of the service.

Narcissists believe that they are never wrong. They seem to know everything better than anyone else. There is no point in arguing with narcissists because even if they are convinced that they are wrong, which is unlikely, it is impossible for them to admit it. They will maintain their position with rational or irrational reasons, or sometimes with no reason at all.

Charles Schulz, the author of the *Peanuts* comic strip, shows us two varieties of people with a negative self-image. The first is Charlie Brown, a pathetic character who fails at everything because he believes he is going to fail and is convinced that he can never do anything right. The second type is Lucy, who is a narcissist and considers herself God's gift to the world. Lucy is domineering, opinionated, and always right.

Peanuts® by Charles M. Schulz. Reprinted by permission of United Feature Syndicate, Inc.

Lucy is infatuated with Schroeder, who ignores her. Lucy nags Schroeder, demanding affection from him, but everything she does only annoys him.

The tragedy with narcissism is that it is self-defeating. Love cannot be given on demand. In fact, the more a person demands to be loved, the less he or she will be loved. Some narcissists are very sensitive and can detect that they are not being loved, and this drives them into a frenzy where they demand it even more. It is obvious that this sets up a vicious cycle that frequently results in emotional and/or physical abuse.

Peanuts® by Charles M. Schulz. Reprinted by permission of United Feature Syndicate, Inc.

Schulz cleverly demonstrates that Lucy's apparent self-adoration is really a desperate attempt to escape the torment of her feeling so poorly about herself.

Lucy is the flip side of Charlie Brown. Her grandiosity is a desperate defense against her negative self-image. When Schroeder says something complimentary toward her, she no longer needs her defensiveness, and her underlying feelings emerge.

Peanuts® by Charles M. Schulz. Reprinted by permission of United Feature Syndicate, Inc.

EIGHT

Fear of Happiness and Fear of Failure

B renda was very anxious, obsessed with a fear that her baby would suffer crib death. "I get up several times during the night to check on her and see if she is breathing. I just dread going over to the crib." Brenda's emotional condition was getting progressively worse by sleep deprivation. It was a vicious cycle.

Brenda had no immediate contact with a case of crib death; her only exposure to it was on television or in magazines. Why, then, was she so anxious? "Because the child is so beautiful, and I know I don't deserve having such a beautiful child."

It is hard to believe that there are people who dread enjoying life. Some people have a sense of foreboding. They are afraid that if they enjoy things, something terrible will happen. Consequently, they consciously or unconsciously torment themselves or deprive themselves of pleasure.

They may feel so undeserving of good fortune that they anticipate misery. Sometimes this is tied to a religious belief in a punitive god who is going to punish them for being bad. Those who think they are bad expect to be punished. Sometimes they do not have a concept of a loving god, or if they do, they may think of themselves as so unworthy that even God could not love them.

Jim had a repetitive problem with alcoholism, and he relapsed after each course of treatment. During one course of treatment it appeared that Jim had turned the corner. There was a marked change in his attitude, and the staff was optimistic that he was sincere about his recovery. Sure enough, several months later Jim was still sober and regularly attended AA meetings. I met him when he was ten months sober and made a note on my calendar to congratulate him on his first year of recovery.

Four days prior to his anniversary, Jim was admitted for detoxification after days of heavy drinking. His appearance was dreadful. He wept, "You've got to believe me, Doc. I didn't enjoy drinking.

"I was approaching a full year of sobriety. I haven't been sober for a single month since age eleven. It was too good to be true. I received a promotion at work, and for the first time I could remember, my wife told me she loved me. I knew it couldn't last and that something terrible was going to happen. Every time the phone rang, I just knew it was to tell me that my little girl had been hit by a car. I couldn't take the suspense. I had to get it over with."

People sabotage themselves in many ways. They climb a ladder, only to topple it as they near the top. We say they are afraid of success. Why would anyone fear success? Because when you don't feel you deserve it, success can produce a great deal of tension.

Medications that are very helpful may have negative side effects. To a person who has a negative self-image, things that should bring about happiness may also have "side ef-

Peanuts® by Charles M. Schulz. Reprinted by permission of United Feature Syndicate, Inc.

fects," and the person may actually do something to precipitate distress.

We can thus see how a negative self-image may lead to a great variety of self-defeating behaviors and that both to function optimally and to enjoy life, a correction of the self-image is essential.

Ernie graduated from accounting school with good grades. Full of enthusiasm, he dressed up in his three-piece suit and took his new briefcase to his first job interview. Although he felt that the session went well, the interviewer told him that they were really looking for someone with a master's degree in business administration.

Ernie returned home not only disappointed but virtually shattered. The following day he did not get out of bed until noon, and that pattern continued. He avoided job interviews, giving various excuses why he could not make them. When his parents prodded him about looking for a job, Ernie began complaining of sundry aches and pains. He made the round of doctors, who could not find any reason for his complaints.

No one likes to fail. However, since we have no assurance of how anything will turn out, we do things with full awareness that we may fail. As painful as failures may be, they should not be devastating. If we do fail, we lick our wounds, learn what we can from the experience, and go on living and trying again.

This may not be true for someone with a negative self-image. Like Charlie Brown, if one is absolutely convinced of failure, there is no purpose in trying.

Peanuts® by Charles M. Schulz. Reprinted by permission of United Feature Syndicate, Inc.

People who perceive a failure as a total devastation don't try anything because the risk of failure is too great. They just drift along, being carried wherever the tide takes them. Although doing nothing results in the greatest failure of all, it is easier for them to accept passive failure than active failure. Furthermore, they can come up with a myriad of rationalizations about why they did not try. They may fantasize that if it had not been for circumstances beyond their control, they would have tried and succeeded.

Those who are unable to retreat into passivity must find other ways to avoid failure. A common mechanism is *perfectionism*. Perfectionists think of all possible causes of failure and then take the necessary steps to prevent them. This is usually impossible to accomplish, and furthermore, the enormous energy spent in closing every gap may leave a person without enough strength to get anything done.

There is no precise line separating appropriate caution from pathologic perfectionism. And there are indeed some situations that require greater caution than normal. Yet there are degrees of perfectionism that are clearly abnormal.

I worked with a nurse who was deathly afraid of making a medication error. She went through a ritual of checking and rechecking medications to the point where medications that were to be dispensed at 7:00 A.M. were not dispensed until after 8:00. After giving a patient the medication, she asked that it be given back to her so that she could make certain it was the right one. She eventually stopped patients from swallowing the medication after it was in their mouths, in order to retrieve it and recheck it. At this point she was dismissed. Her perfectionism resulted in the ultimate failure: the loss of her job.

"Reasonable" perfectionism is just that: perfection

guided by reason. When perfectionism is not guided by reason but is subject to emotion, it may know no bounds, particularly when the dominant emotion is fear of making a mistake. What is "just a mistake" to many people and accepted as one of the unavoidable components of life can be a devastating experience to a person with a negative self-image. A mistake can be a confirmation of feelings of unworth. Living can become a terrifying experience.

I was once riding in a car with a friend, and we were listening to a tape of a recovering alcoholic who described his earlier years as "feeling like I was walking through a minefield, where the next step might blow me to bits." My friend brought the car to a screeching halt and broke out in a cold sweat. "I never thought anyone else felt like that," he said.

Many people feel that way. Their negative self-concept leads them to believe that they are going to fail, and a failure is indeed confirmation of their worst fears about themselves. These fears may generate intense anticipatory anxiety, which may then be the cause of failure. I refer to this as the "William Tell Phenomenon."

According to the legend, William Tell was an excellent archer who was ordered to shoot at an apple perched on his son's head, and indeed succeeded. If any archer other than Tell had been told to aim at an ordinary bull's-eye, he might well hit it. But he might not. In any event, his hand would be steady, since there would be nothing at stake to generate anxiety. The worst that could happen would be to miss the bull's-eye. However, if like Tell he had to shoot an apple off his child's head, the dread of missing the apple and harming the child would be so devastating that he could not possibly hold the bow steady, and any chance of shooting accurately would be doomed.

A disproportionate fear of failing may generate so much anxiety that success is impossible. This is why people with scant self-confidence may fail at challenges that are well within their range.

NINE

Compartmentalization

S ome people have a negative self-image that is global:
They think negatively of themselves in every way. Others have a partial distortion of their self-perception: They
recognize some of the positives about themselves but negatively distort other aspects of their personality.

Dr. Brown spent most of his waking hours in either the
hospital or the office, weekends included. He began his
hospital rounds early in the morning, went to the office in
the afternoon, and returned to the hospital until late at
night. He was a teacher par excellence, greatly admired by
the house staff, students, and nurses, and his patients virtually adored him. Some of the nurses commented that the
reason he spent all his time in the hospital was to avoid his
home. They assumed that his wife must be a shrew.

One day I received a call from Dr. Brown, who asked me
to see his wife about her depression. I was rather surprised
to meet a woman who was the epitome of kindness and
gentleness, nothing like what the nurses had pictured. In
relating the factors she felt had contributed to her depression, she said, "You know my husband, how dedicated he

is to medicine. Well, I'm an insecure person, and I always needed a shoulder to rest my head on, but he was never there for me. Our children grew up without a father. Oh, yes, if they were sick he took excellent care of them, but he was their doctor rather than a father."

I subsequently interviewed her husband, whom I knew to be not only a first-rate physician but also a wonderful person. It came to light that he thought poorly of himself as a person. His negative self-concept did not extend to his profession, but as a human being, he felt he was inadequate.

"He doesn't know his name, just that he's a Doctor."
Copyright © 1994 by Ed Stein.

Dr. Brown was comfortable at the hospital and at the office because he felt adequate as a doctor. At home he had to function as a person providing emotional support for his wife and guidance for the children. Because he felt inadequate in this latter role, he avoided it.

If, on a stifling hot summer day, we have access to two

rooms, one of which is air-conditioned, we will certainly choose the more comfortable room. It is a law of nature that living things gravitate to the most comfortable surroundings.

For Dr. Brown the hospital and office were comfortable. Home was uncomfortable, not because his family was too demanding or inconsiderate, but because he felt he lacked what the family needed.

Like many other people who spend excessive hours at the office, Dr. Brown was able to deceive himself that his professional responsibilities demanded these hours. This was not true for him, and it is not true for many others who do not spend enough time with their families.

There are probably more "compartmentalized" people than we imagine. Ask a person who he is, and he is likely to tell you what he *does*. Not too many people respond with "I am a gentle, soft-spoken person. I enjoy reading, and I am a nature lover." Many more people say that they are an accountant or legal secretary or computer analyst. Their identity is essentially tied to what they do. Their sense of self is very limited.

A dancer sought psychiatric consultation for depression. In describing the pervasive feelings of dejection that had plagued her since childhood, she noticeably brightened when she talked about performing. "That's when the true me comes out." Since she performed only several hours a week, her "true self" appeared for only a small fraction of her life. For the greater part of the week she was morose. She had no knowledge of her true self, only a mistaken concept from which she escaped when she performed skillfully. She was a classic example of "look at what I *do,* not at what I *am.*"

A schoolteacher whose marriage had deteriorated because of his emotional abusiveness refused to accept my suggestion that his behavior was related to his low self-esteem. It was clear that he sought to reinforce his sagging self-concept by exercising his authority as master of the house. "I do not have poor self-esteem," he said. "I am an excellent teacher, and I have been selected several times by the students in the school as the best teacher on the staff. Parents are invariably thrilled when they find out their children are in my class." Like the doctor and the dancer, his identity was as a teacher, not as a person. Since he could not do any teaching with his wife, he felt bankrupt in her presence. Although his behavior at school was exemplary, his behavior at home was intolerable. As a good teacher, he would listen, teach, and relate with a feeling of self-confidence. As a husband, he felt unworthy and reacted defensively by adopting an overbearing attitude.

A positive self-image allows us to be good spouses and parents. A negative self-image deprives us of the love we can both give and receive.

TEN

Depression

People with feelings of inferiority are likely to feel depressed. To alleviate this depression, they must correct their self-image. It is important, however, that the type of self-image distortion be identified, because it is possible that it is a *consequence* of depression rather than a cause, and that treatment with medication may be necessary along with psychotherapy.

We now know that there are a variety of chemical changes that can produce depression. A number of medications, both prescribed and over the counter, can cause depression. Among these are decongestants, frequently used for relief of sinus conditions, hay fever, or the common cold; some appetite suppressants; and some antihistamines, especially if taken more often than recommended. It is also possible for internal bodily changes such as hepatitis, infectious mononucleosis, or any severe viral illness, a surgical procedure, or the hormonal changes of the premenstrual, postpartum, or menopausal phases to result in depression. Sleep disturbance can result in depression, and it is possible for depression to be of genetic origin. A grief reaction following a personal loss can progress into a clinical depression, but it is important to be aware that severe depression can be based solely on a biochemical change.

The symptoms of severe depression may include loss of sleep, loss of appetite, loss of interest in things, loss of sex drive, crying, inability to concentrate, despair, and death wishes. These feelings are generally accompanied by *intense feelings of worthlessness and inadequacy*, the feelings comprising low self-esteem.

It is important to recognize that in this situation, the feelings of worthlessness and inferiority may be secondary to a depression of biochemical origin. When the depression is relieved with proper treatment, the feelings of worthlessness may disappear. A person who had a very positive self-image may develop a severely negative self-image due to a clinical depression. When the depression is appropriately treated, the positive self-image returns.

One of the distinguishing features between depression due to a negative self-image and clinical depression is that the latter almost invariably has an onset. The person "felt fine until about eight months ago." When depression stems from feelings of inferiority, it has generally been a part of that individual's personality for as long as anyone can remember. The problem is that during clinical depression, a person may be looking at life through smoked glass. He sees the past, present, and future as all being bleak. He may very well say, "I felt this way about myself since I can remember," which may not be true. Family members may be able to provide more accurate information about when the negative feelings occurred.

We do not yet have a laboratory test that can diagnose clinical depression. When in doubt, it may be wise to get treatment for the clinical depression, and then one can direct attention to the feelings of inferiority from a negative self-image. Trying to deal with a negative self-image in the presence of an untreated clinical depression can result in the development of many misleading misconceptions.

People suffering with depression may develop feelings of hopelessness, and if they do not see any light at the end of the tunnel, they may attempt suicide. If they can be helped to an awareness that their perception of reality is not accurate, and be given hope that things can turn out much better than they expect, this tragedy can be averted.

Paul is an attorney who was thirty-six years old when he consulted me for treatment of his depression. He admitted that he had been seriously contemplating suicide.

After listening to his description of how everything in life had gone wrong for him, I asked Paul whether he had ever made a concerted effort at getting to know himself, or whether he had just taken himself for granted without any self-examination. When he stated that he had never really done any serious introspection, I pointed out to him that in all likelihood he lacked true self-awareness. I reminded Paul that just a few weeks earlier there had been an account in the news of a man who went berserk and killed several people at random in a busy shopping center.

"What do you think about a person like that?" I asked.

"He must be insane," Paul said. "Why would anyone kill people he doesn't even know?"

I then pointed out to Paul that inasmuch as he lacked self-awareness, he was in fact a stranger to himself, and although he felt depressed, this did not give him an excuse to kill a stranger. To do so would be as irrational as the person who went berserk in the shopping center. I told Paul that regardless of how depressed he felt, the idea of suicide would have to be delayed until he had a valid self-awareness. Once the latter was achieved, we could then discuss the entire issue of suicide. Paul actually smiled at the idea.

Paul entered group therapy directed at self-awareness and self-esteem enhancement. Two years later I received a letter from him stating that he had come to know himself much better and that suicide was absolutely the last thing he would consider. "I like this guy too much to think of killing him."

Estelle was depressed following the birth of her third child. Her second child, who was at that time seven, had a serious hearing deficit, and Estelle was determined to mainstream the child rather than have him in special education classes. She devoted a great deal of attention to this child, but now she had a baby to attend to as well. When she entered treatment she appeared physically exhausted. She considered herself an inadequate mother because she was unable to respond to all the needs of her children.

Estelle required some medication for the depression, and she also entered into a therapy group. Here she was helped to see that she was dealing very adequately with some major challenges of parenting. The group encouraged her to try and get additional help so that she could devote her attention to her children without overtaxing her capacities. As her depression lifted and her self-esteem improved, Estelle functioned very well and did succeed in mainstreaming her child in school.

We all have off days, and there are many circumstances in life that can cause us to feel depressed. However, when symptoms of depression persist or become disabling, we need to seek competent treatment.

ELEVEN

Anxiety

Anxiety is another condition that can be caused by either psychological or biochemical factors. Appropriate medication is often necessary for biochemical anxiety.

A word of caution is necessary here. There are many antianxiety medications. However, like alcohol, these medications relieve anxiety by depressing the brain so that the person is less sensitive. The problem with these medications is that their effect lasts for only several hours. Many people become immune to them. They then take increasing doses to eliminate the anxiety, and since most of these medications are potentially addictive, they may develop severe addictions. When this happens, the person has a complicated problem: addiction on top of chronic anxiety.

Anxiety is a feeling very similar to fear. However, in fear there is a threatening situation. A person concerned about a medical condition may feel threatened by an undesirable diagnosis. In anxiety there are no apparent threats. Common feelings of anxiety include a sensation of impending doom and/or palpitation, shortness of breath, chest pain, and dizziness. These symptoms may occur in varying degrees of intensity. Such sensations may result from physical causes, such as certain medications, especially decongestants and caffeine, low blood sugar, or thyroid disease. Very severe and sudden anxiety attacks are called panic attacks, and it is believed that some of these are caused by a biochemical imbalance similar to that which may cause depression. Anxiety may also exist in a chronic, low-key form.

The psychological causes of anxiety are not always evident. Some psychologists postulate that there may be an unconscious threat; the person is afraid of something but is not aware of what it is. Sometimes there are no physical sensations; the person feels haunted, like something terrible is going to happen. Not knowing what it is, he or she has no way of controlling or avoiding it.

A negative self-image is often a component of anxiety. A person who is secure and self-confident is not likely to feel overwhelmed by the challenges in life. But a person with feelings of inadequacy is understandably more vulnerable to anxiety. Recall the man who described himself as feeling as though he were walking through a minefield. Although with each step he realized that he had thus far been safe, this did not diminish his fear that the next step would result in an explosion. In addition to increased fear, a person with the negative self-image may also be reluctant to seek outside help, seeing this as an admission of weakness.

Barbara is an attorney who consulted a psychiatrist because of severe panic attacks. In the absence of any threatening circumstances, Barbara would develop heart palpitation, tightness of the chest, shortness of breath, and dizziness. Her doctor prescribed a medication that significantly reduced the frequency and severity of the attacks, but Barbara was left with a pervasive feeling of anxiety. She was afraid to drive, so her husband drove her to and from work. She felt fairly secure at home or in the office, but other situations intensified her anxiety, and she essentially avoided all other activities, remaining in the security of home or office.

Barbara was offered a promotion at work, but this would entail periodic trips out of town, which she could not consider because of her anxiety. She therefore consulted a psychologist for behavior modification treatment. The psychologist correctly concluded that Barbara's anxiety was related to feelings of inadequacy, although her academic and work careers had attested to her competence. In addition to practicing behavior modification techniques, Barbara entered group therapy.

Barbara's low self-esteem was intensified by her inability to function away from the security of the home or office. Her anxiety, which was partially due to feelings of inadequacy, thus intensified her feelings of inadequacy, resulting in a vicious cycle.

The group therapy helped Barbara gain a better sense of herself, and with the encouragment and support of the group she began venturing out of her home and office. Each successful trip improved her self-esteem, and the negative vicious cycle was replaced by a positive, self-reinforcing pattern. Barbara eventually accepted the promotion, and she is able to travel without fear or anxiety.

Bob is a successful financial adviser who stuttered as a child. He eventually overcame the problem, but he still avoids speaking before groups, since this reactivates his stutter. Bob's firm began giving seminars on financial planning, and Bob's job assignment now required speaking in front of rather large groups. Bob tried to prevent his anxiety from provoking the stutter by taking tranquilizers, but these made him drowsy and interfered with his presentation.

Bob was a child of an abusive, alcoholic father, and his early life was replete with trauma. The psychologist he consulted decided not to dwell on the origins of the anxiety but rather on the consequences of the traumatic childhood—his consequent low self-esteem. Bob had come to anticipate failure, and each time he had to speak before a group he was apprehensive that he would blurt out something stupid and be sharply criticized for it.

Group therapy was selected as the most effective treatment method. As Bob came to a better self-awareness, his anticipation of failure decreased, and he was eventually able to speak successfully in front of large groups. Interestingly, this had a ripple effect: His business activities, social activities, and even family situation improved greatly.

No one knows what the future holds. Life is full of surprises, some pleasant, others unpleasant. The more adequate we feel, the less threatening the unknown stresses become. I have noted that people with negative self-images may have greater expectations of unpleasant things happening to them. They have a twofold problem: expecting trouble and not feeling competent to cope with it. As the next chapter shows, this may contribute to the development of alcoholism or other addictions.

TWELVE

Alcoholism and
Other Chemical Addictions

Addiction to alcohol or to other mood-altering chemicals can take various shapes and forms, and we still aren't sure why some people develop addictions and others do not. There is undoubtedly a genetic vulnerability in some people, but genetics alone does not account for these conditions.

There are obviously some psychological factors involved in addiction, and one of them is negative self-image. I'm not referring to the feelings of inferiority that result from being addicted to alcohol and/or drugs, although there are an abundance of these. Virtually all addicted people had a negative self-image *prior* to becoming involved with alcohol or other drugs. Here's a typical account given by a surgeon, now more than thirty years sober. "I did not take my first drink until I was seventeen, and I did not start my heavy drinking until I was twenty-six. But I can clearly remember when I was nine years old, feeling that I was different from all the other kids and that they were better than I was." These feelings of inadequacy and inferiority preceded his drinking by many years. I have yet to meet an alcoholic or drug-addicted person who had a positive self-image prior to becoming addicted.

In Chapter 1, I noted one reason why a negative self-image is conducive to addiction: The natural resistance to ruining an item of value is absent in a person who does not see himself or herself as valuable. A second important factor is a person's feelings about his or her competence to cope with challenges.

There are only two possible ways of dealing with any challenge in life: coping or escaping. There is no third option. Ignoring a problem is simply a passive way of escaping.

In some situations the correct action is to escape. If your automobile is stalled on the railroad tracks and you see a train approaching at 120 miles per hour, this is not the time or place to cope. Escape is appropriate because the challenge is overwhelming. A 180-pound person is no match for a 60-ton diesel.

We can break reactions down into a simple formula: If the challenge is much greater than you, escape. If you are greater than the challenge, cope. If you appear to be about equal, or if the challenge appears to be only a bit greater, enlist some outside help.

Although this formula seems elementary, many people choose not to cope with life's challenges. Why? The decision whether to cope or escape ultimately depends on how we size up ourselves in comparison to the challenge. In the case of the diesel engine, we decide to escape because the challenge is too great. In cases where the challenge is in reality not overwhelming, we may feel overwhelmed if we see ourselves as not having the capacity to cope. Depending on how inadequate we feel, we may escape from many challenges that are perfectly within our capacity.

Of the many methods of escape, one of the most common is to numb one's feelings with chemicals. Many people use alcohol or other chemicals to try to render themselves oblivious to their problems. Of course, reality problems that are ignored rarely evaporate. To the contrary, they usually get worse, making escapist tactics even more likely in the future.

It is unfortunate that there is a cultural ethos that encourages pathological escapism. The media bombard us with the idea that we should use chemicals to escape from problems. A commercial recommends that if you feel tense after a day's work, you should take an over-the-counter tranquilizer. But feeling tense after a harrowing day at work is a perfectly normal response that does not require any medication. A number of years ago, the manufacturer of a tranquilizer ran a commercial in which a woman discovered that her sink drain was clogged on the day she was to serve a special dinner for her husband's boss. In desperation she turned to her friend for help. Instead of suggesting calling a plumber, the friend recommended taking this tranquilizer to allay her anxiety. This is the message of addiction.

In one of my lectures at our rehabilitation center, I used this commercial as an illustration. Several months later I received a letter from a woman who had undergone treatment at our center for a combined alcohol and tranquilizer addiction. She wrote that she wanted to demonstrate her new efficiency in recovery and invited sixteen people to a New Year's dinner. On New Year's Day she discovered that her sink drain was clogged, and her husband could not get it unclogged. Since it was New Year's Day, getting a plumber was impossible.

"My husband looked at me with grave concern. In my

drinking days, a much lesser stress would have sent me to the bottle. But I remembered your lecture, and I just burst into laughter.

"We used the sink in the powder room to wash vegetables and prepare the food, and after dinner the guests helped me carry the dishes down to the laundry tub in the basement and even volunteered to wash them. We had a great time. I can only think of the disaster that would have resulted if this had happened before I was in recovery."

Using medication to relieve average workday tension is never advisable. This tension is best dealt with by jogging, listening to music, handiwork, reading a book, relaxation exercises, and so on. Escaping from tension by depressing the alertness of the brain with alcohol or other chemicals is counterproductive and may lead to addiction. Medications should be reserved for illnesses, and even then used carefully to avoid addiction. Certainly where there is no illness, there is no need for medication.

The idea behind these commercials is an insult to our intelligence. We are capable of coping with clogged-up drains, work tension, and many other problems. We are capable of surviving the normal tensions of life and dissipating them with healthful measures. To tell us to use chemicals for relief is demeaning. Unfortunately, people with negative self-images are highly susceptible to the seduction of these messages.

In recovering from addiction, you learn more about yourself and discover coping capabilities of which you were unaware. This is one of the excellent steps advocated by the twelve-step fellowships such as Alcoholics Anonymous and Narcotics Anonymous. The fourth and fifth steps require making a thorough, painstaking inventory of yourself and sharing it with another person. Repeating this process helps eliminate many negative misconceptions. Accepting guidance from a sponsor provides an objective perspective, which further helps correct the distorted perspective, and in this way you gradually overcome your negative attitude toward yourself. A similar program of self-awareness is very helpful in correcting an erroneous self-concept and can serve as a preventative measure to avoid development of addictions that are the result of escapist maneuvers.

THIRTEEN

Eating Disorders

Eating disorders, particularly compulsive eating and bulimia, have some resemblance to alcoholism and drug addiction. Eating should provide the body with necessary nutrition, and hunger is the body's way of notifying us that we need food. When the body's nutritive needs are satisfied, hunger should disappear. Craving for food after the body's needs have been met is not healthy hunger but a result of something gone awry in the body.

Imagine coming home, turning on the light switch, and discovering that instead of the lights going on, the garbage disposal was activated. Clearly there has been a cross-up in the wiring, so you call an electrician to untangle the system.

Hunger should be activated only by the body's nutritional needs. When something else activates hunger, this indicates of a cross-up in the body's wiring. Food is supplying something other than nutrition. It's like activating the garbage disposal when you want the lights on.

A cross-up is likely to occur when the system is in some type of distress: depression, anger, anxiety, loneliness, envy, or other unpleasant emotions. Somehow, the signals got mixed up and the body is calling for food to relieve the discomfort. Food then becomes a kind of drug, much like alcohol. It makes no difference what type of food it is; it doesn't have to be sugary or starchy. *Food that is not for nutritive purposes is a drug.* Virtually everything that has been said about alcohol or other mind-altering chemicals can be said about nonnutritive food intake.

As with chemical dependency, low self-esteem is found in virtually every person with an eating disorder. For the person with an eating disorder, the relationship with food becomes a substitute for relationships with people. The reason for turning to food instead of cultivating relationships is often due to a feeling of low self-worth, so the person may despair of having a meaningful relationship. "Why should anyone like someone like me?"

To people with low self-esteem, relationships are unreliable. "If the person I like ever gets to know me, he won't like me anymore." Food becomes a substitute for relationships because it is totally reliable. Food never rejects you.

As I mentioned earlier, people with low self-esteem are reluctant to acknowledge their neediness and their dependence on others. By turning to food instead of to other people, they maintain denial of their neediness.

As with alcohol, escaping into eating often leads to a vicious cycle. The low self-worth that initiates the eating disorder becomes aggravated as you lose control over food and either binge or gain too much weight. The guilty feelings generated by overindulgence make you feel even worse about yourself, causing further escape into food.

Food can become a tranquilizer in a variety of ways. It is possible that in some people there are physiological reasons. We know that the brain produces chemicals known as endorphins, which give a person a pleasurable sensation.

There is reason to believe that in some people food intake stimulates endorphin production, and it has been postulated that in anorexia, loss of weight does the same thing. Some anorexics have described a rush with weight loss that is similar to what a drug addicts describe as a chemical high.

For some people, food became a manifestation of love early in life. Parents who lacked self-esteem may have felt that they were not giving their children enough. As one young mother said, "I give myself totally to my children, but so what? They still have nothing." In such instances it is not unusual for parents to try to compensate by giving the children food, which then becomes symbolic of parental love. This impression is carried into later life. If you do not feel deserving of love from any other source, you may turn to food.

Earlier I explained how people with low self-esteem may have a fear of success. This is also a frequent occurrence in eating disorders and may explain the yo-yo phenomenon of weight loss and gain. To some people, maintaining the weight loss is an intolerable success!

Eating disorders are self-defeating. They may drain your energies so much that little strength remains for advancement. They are often aesthetically disfiguring, and they certainly are physically unhealthful.

Part III

Turning on the Power of Self-Esteem

FOURTEEN

Self-Assessment and Support: The Road to Recovery

I have described the problems that are caused by low self-esteem. Now what is the solution? How do we develop a positive self-image? It is by no means simple, but it can be accomplished.

The first step is accepting the possibility that our self-concept is invalid. Otherwise there is no possibility of any change. We have no motivation to make a self-assessment if we already know ourselves. Furthermore, why would we bother to search through a pile of rubble if we are convinced it contains nothing of value? We must have reason to believe that there is something of value to be found in order to make the effort.

It is not easy to shed convictions about one's self-image. If it is correct that the negative self-image begins in childhood, then a person who begins a self-assessment in middle age must be ready to let go of ideas that he or she has harbored for forty or more years. There is great resistance in relinquishing ideas that have been deeply entrenched for so long.

The second step is to make lifestyle changes that promote

a more positive self-image, and there may be fierce resistance to this. We are creatures of habit, and most of us are reluctant to change established patterns.

When lecturing on this theme, I often ask the audience to fold their arms across their chest and note whether they habitually cross the left arm over the right or vice versa. I then suggest they do it the opposite way and report how they feel. People invariably report an awkwardness in folding their arms in the opposite way, and they cannot maintain that position for an extended period of time without discomfort. If altering a simple posture is fraught with discomfort, imagine how distressful it is to alter significant behaviors. The tendency to return to a familiar, well-established pattern because it is more comfortable often inhibits the drive to develop an altered self-image.

The third step is to be extremely patient. A self-image that has prevailed for the greater part of our life is not going to be replaced quickly. Changes in self-concept are gradual and come in small increments. Relapses into the old self-concept are frequent. It may take years before there are substantive changes in self-image.

If these three conditions are satisfied, we can begin a self-assessment. Doing this alone may be of limited value. We have been looking at ourselves through distorting lenses and are not likely to see anything different if we look again. Nevertheless, some progress may be made, and there is no harm in trying to do it on our own.

Let's begin with the premise of this book, "I am better than I think I am." A sculptor finished a masterpiece, and when an observer marveled at his artistry, he said, "It really wasn't that great an accomplishment. I saw the statue inside the slab of marble, and all I had to do was chip away the pieces so that it could be visible to everyone." Knowing that there is a great deal of good inside ourselves makes the job simpler.

Now let's look at what gives a person value. Our feeling good about ourselves is related to our unique human aspects, our character and personality. Some of the unique human character traits are love, honesty, courage, humility, generosity, and empathy. It is safe to assume that we all possess these, and if they have not been manifest in our lives, it is because they have been concealed. Like the sculpture, we need to expose them.

One major difference between people and animals is that we can make intelligent choices based on concepts of right and wrong, good and bad, rather than having our behavior determined by whatever it is the body craves. To the degree that we make intelligent choices and exercise our unique human traits, we gain pride and self-esteem.

Keep in mind that making intelligent choices may not initially give us as comfortable a lifestyle as that of following our urges and drives. In other words, gaining self-esteem may require sacrificing some of the things we are attracted to. But it is a price well worth paying.

Self-esteem requires trust in ourselves. Co-dependent people do not trust their own impressions and judgments and continually look for cues in how other people react to them. Are they smiling and appear to be approving, or does a frown indicate disapproval?

It is wise to seek advice from others. When we talk about a problem, we often discover facets of which we had been unaware. Our own clear understanding and the perspective of an objective person can help us make better judgments, but this is different from being dependent on other people for every choice or decision. Although we should be flexible, we should begin making our own decisions and trusting our own opinions. If we make mistakes, these can be positive learning experiences, not devastating failures.

We all make mistakes. Some are costly, and we have every reason to regret them. But the function of regret should be to alert us not to repeat these mistakes, rather than self-condemnation. We learn many important things in life by experience. The proverb "Experience is a hard teacher, but fools will learn no other way" is wrong. Fools are those who fail to learn from experience. If you have made a mistake, even a serious one, and you have learned not to repeat it, then you are wise.

Obtaining a positive self-image means dispensing with the old one. It is easy to act out of habit; thinking how we are going to act takes effort. It is clear, however, that development of a new self-image requires a break with the past. It is only natural to follow the path of least resistance and revert to old, well-established patterns. So we must remain on guard and keep our wits about us, welcoming opportunities for constructive change.

Trusting ourselves allows us to be assertive, not necessarily aggressive, but appropriately assertive. Assertiveness gradually replaces pathological withdrawal and allows us to advance. Such progress reinforces self-trust, putting into motion a positive self-reinforcing cycle.

A young woman consulted me at the urging of a friend who had told her, "Cathy, you are letting life pass you by. You've got to see someone for help."

Cathy was thirty-eight, a charming woman who held a clerical position in a university. She had had this job for eleven years and had consistently assumed more responsibilities. She recognized that she was doing the work of three people. However, she had never asked for a promotion.

Cathy's social life was nil. Her only relationship was

with a married man who saw her at his whim. Although he said that he loved her, there was no indication that he intended to make their relationship permanent. She was frustrated playing second fiddle to the wife whom he said he did not love, but she did not assert herself to establish her position as the woman he truly loved. It was clear that Cathy held on to this relationship because she felt unlovable, and it was too risky to jeopardize a relationship with the one person who said he loved her. If she made him choose between his wife and her, she was certain he would reject her and then she would be totally alone, without hope of finding anyone else.

After eleven years, Cathy did not have any friends from work. Her office was at the far end of a long corridor, in a rather forsaken cul-de-sac where there was no traffic. No one came without some very specific business. Cathy had never made an effort to have her office moved to a more congenial spot.

Cathy brought her lunch from home and ate in her office. When I asked her why she didn't eat in the university cafeteria or in any of the restaurants near the campus, she replied, "Everybody has their own friends at their tables, and nobody wants a stranger imposing upon them."

Cathy could not see that she had effectively isolated herself from people and that her loneliness was largely self-inflicted. The therapeutic breakthrough occurred when I had to cancel an appointment with her, and I couldn't find her phone number. The directory assistance operator told me that Cathy's number was unlisted.

At the next appointment I asked Cathy why she needed an unlisted number. Her rationalizations were very poor, and I was able to show her how far her efforts at isolating herself had gone. Having an unlisted phone number kept her from being contacted by anyone, and like any other defense mechanism, it also permitted her to fantasize, "If people were able to contact me they certainly would. The reason they aren't is only because my number is unlisted." But Cathy was really convinced that her phone would not ring. A silent phone with a listed number would confirm her fear that she was undesirable company. By having her number unlisted, she did not have to deal with this stress.

I outlined several steps Cathy was to take. (1) She would have her phone number listed in the directory. (2) She would no longer eat lunch in her office but go to the cafeteria and approach a table where there was an empty seat and ask, "May I join you?" (3) She would try to relocate her office to an area that was less isolated. (4) She would approach her boss with the well-documented evidence that the work she was doing justified a promotion and possibly a secretary to assist her. (5) She would let her gentleman friend know that she did not plan to continue being his plaything. She did not wish to break up his marriage, but she was looking for a serious, long-term commitment. If this was not his intention, she did not wish their relationship to continue.

Cathy didn't have to make all these changes at once. First she listed her phone number, which was not much of a problem. She had difficulty approaching a table of strangers in the cafeteria, but finally she did ask and was pleasantly surprised when the people welcomed her. She continued to feel awkward approaching, but she persevered and eventually struck up conversations and made friends with many people.

Cathy's request for a promotion was granted without any hassle, and shortly after that she had her office moved.

She began to attend more university functions and eventually began to date other men. Then she terminated the relationship with the married man.

All of these changes came about gradually and were very painstaking, extending over two years. There were numerous rationalizations that Cathy presented to avoid challenging her symptoms, and various other types of resistances.

It is a good idea to write down things we don't like about ourselves. No change is possible until we identify what it is that we wish to change. Once we identify a behavior or feeling, we can begin by making a change "just for today." As Lao-tzu wisely noted two thousand years ago, "A journey of a thousand miles must begin with a single step."

For example, perhaps you don't like your passivity and your failure to stand up for your rights or assert your opinion. Decide that for the next twenty-four hours you will be on the alert to practice self-assertion. You may find that at work someone takes something of yours without asking, because this is how you have trained him. Today you will say, "Pardon me, Bill, but I may have to use this now. If you need it, please ask for it." Or if your husband leaves the table without removing the dishes, you say, "Honey, it's your turn to do the dishes tonight." Such remarks coming from you may elicit a quizzical reaction. You have to do this only today. Tomorrow you will consider tomorrow's tactics.

The "Serenity Prayer," written by the theologian Reinhold Niebuhr and adopted by AA, has two components: accepting things we cannot change and changing things we can. We must accept the past; it cannot be changed. But acceptance does not mean approval. I can accept that I have been a certain way, but I need not approve of this and I can muster the courage to change.

Change need not be radical. In fact, radical changes are rarely helpful. We must accommodate to changes and give others the opportunity to accommodate. Changes should preferably be in small increments.

Nathaniel Branden, a pioneer in self-esteem psychology, recommends completing sentences such as, What I like most about myself is . . . What I like least about myself is . . . I would like to be . . . I am happiest when . . . , and to review these sentences, making gradual changes to eliminate negative qualities and to implement positive traits. This can be a beginning of building self-esteem.

There is no denying that past events have an impact on how we perceive and value ourselves, but it is important to realize that nothing is cast in stone. With a bit of determination and effort, we can make changes.

Frequently we are unaware of unwarranted feelings of inadequacy that obstruct our progress or interfere with relationships. I have used the psychological insights of cartoonist Charles Schulz, who so clearly illustrates Charlie Brown's resignation to failure, Lucy's defense of belittling everyone, and Snoopy's flight into fantasy, in my previous books *When Do the Good Things Start?* and *Waking Up Just in Time.* It may be helpful to amuse yourself by reading these strips, and while smiling at these lovable characters jot down the traits you can identify in yourself.

Identifying our negative self-image symptoms and confronting them is only a small step. The problem is that without urging and support, we are likely to revert to our previous behavior, justifying it by rationalizations.

This is why it is generally necessary to have the help of an outside observer, preferably a counselor or therapist who is qualified to detect distortions in self-perception.

Not all psychotherapists are well suited to address a negative self-image problem. Some who are deeply rooted in psychodynamic theories may not have the proper approach for correcting a negative self-image.

I discovered this myself early in my psychiatric career. In medical school, we spent the first year studying anatomy, biochemistry, physiology, and human tissues. That marked our last contact with anything normal. The remainder of our education was focused on pathology: tumors, disease-causing bacteria and viruses, trauma, and abnormalities in physiology. Our thinking became pathology-oriented, and whenever we were confronted with a person with symptoms, our thoughts took the direction of looking for what was wrong with the person.

When I became a psychiatrist, I continued to look for what had gone wrong with my patients. The psychodynamic theories I was taught reinforced this approach. I searched through my patients' experiences, all the way back to their early childhoods, to find the source of the pathology. The idea was that if the patient realized the source of the symptoms and this could be extirpated, the symptoms would disappear.

The theory sounds logical, but I was disappointed in the results. Patients often said, "I understand everything thoroughly, Doctor, but I don't feel any better."

I then came to a realization that I later found was encapsulated by Charles Schulz in four simple frames.

People are composed of thoughts and feelings, which is the "inner self," and also of actions and behavior, which can be considered the "outer self." Others cannot know what goes on inside us, because our thoughts and feelings are private. What people see is our actions and behavior. Furthermore, even though we know at least some of our own thoughts and feelings, we are probably more affected by what we do than by what we think.

Peanuts® by Charles M. Schulz. Reprinted by permission of United Feature Syndicate, Inc.

In this comic strip, Schulz is telling us that changing our thoughts and feelings may have little impact on our behavior. Sally's "outer obnoxiousness" really indicates that she never had any true "inner peace." Behaving with courtesy and consideration to others is more likely to result in inner peace than inner peace resulting in more pleasant behavior. Modern psychologists, many of whom belong to one of the behaviorist schools, therefore advocate changing behavior first, working from the outside in.

As I became involved in the treatment of alcoholism, I noted the striking difference in approach between traditional psychotherapists who treated alcoholics and the Alcoholics Anonymous program. The psychotherapists focused on searching for the reason why a person drank and most often ended up with a person who had a good understanding why he or she was still getting drunk. Alcoholic Anonymous focused on the disturbed behavior: "Don't pick up the first drink, and get yourself to meetings," and these results were much more impressive.

"Oh, no! Not another self-esteem problem!"

Cartoon by Bill Hoest. Copyright Wm. Hoest Enterprises, Inc. Reprinted with permission.

How would the above patient be approached? A traditional psychodynamic psychotherapist would continue to work with the patient "lying under the couch" (not to be taken literally) in the hope that the patient would eventually develop sufficient self-esteem to be able to lie *on* the couch. A much more effective approach is to have the patient lie on the couch and stipulate that unless the patient does so, the therapist will not treat him. Either the patient is allowed to continue his destructive behavior until the magical insight eliminates it, or he can be helped to challenge the symptom and allow the dynamics to be worked out afterward.

The best way to treat a negative self-image is first to alter the behavior that is a manifestation of the distorted self-concept: The loner should begin mixing with people; the people-pleaser should learn how to say no when it is appropriate; the anxiety-ridden person should be encouraged to proceed even in situations that are stressful; the passive person should be helped to become more assertive. All the behaviors that the therapist has identified as being products of the negative self-image must be changed. The role of the therapist is to give the client the necessary support to make these difficult and anxiety-provoking changes and encourage him or her to do so.

Group therapy has advantages over one-to-one therapy in self-image problems. In spite of the ubiquity of the negative self-image, many people think that no one else feels as they do. The awareness that we are not alone is in itself uplifting. Also, knowing other admirable people who have unwarranted feelings of inadequacy may help us realize that we too may be oblivious to our own assets. Finally, the support in making difficult behavioral changes, sharing these experiences, and encouraging others to be assertive and act positively is of inestimable value.

A combination of group therapy and individual therapy may be particularly effective in ridding oneself of unwarranted feelings of shame. For example, a woman who harbors intense feelings of shame and resentment because of being sexually molested as a child may not be able to talk about it in a group. Yet simply relating the incident and even discussing her feelings with the therapist may not alleviate these painful emotions. A therapist utilizing the Gestalt technique might suggest that she pretend that the person who assaulted her is sitting in the other chair and encourage her to express her feelings toward that person. Or the therapist may suggest that she visualize herself as a little girl and express her feelings toward the child, as well as speak for the child. These techniques mobilize much more emotion and can be more effective than simply talking about the experience.

In group therapy, a number of people meet with a therapist. The therapist has generally interviewed participants and identified the particular problems that need correction. The group has a great deal of freedom in discussing various issues, although the therapist may set limitations on which issues will be dealt with in the group. The therapist is likely to offer interpretations of what is happening in the group process, and with professional help, very profound emotional issues may be analyzed.

Self-help groups are a bit different. People get together to exchange life experiences and what they have learned from them.

A group consists of preferably between six and ten people who wish to focus on self-realization and self-actualization. The sine qua non for such a group is a pledge of confidentiality and secrecy, so that members feel free to discuss important emotional issues. The group may choose any of the books on self-esteem as a text, and members take turns reading paragraphs aloud. After each paragraph, members are encouraged to discuss their own experiences. The first few sessions are apt to be rather sterile, since people have not yet gained a sufficient trust in one another to feel free to talk about intimate issues. As sessions continue, there is a gradual thawing, and soon any one sentence of the book may stimulate a meaningful discussion, with free exchanges of ideas and feelings. It is not necessary to have a professional psychologist involved regularly, but it is advisable to have a competent group therapist sit in at an occasional meeting to observe and recommend how the group can maximize its efficiency. Spouses or other close relatives should not be in the same group, since this may result in a reluctance to discuss feelings that concern them. Close friends are also apt to have feelings that they might conceal from each other but would reveal to strangers. They too should not be in the same group.

How do such groups begin? In community lectures on the subject of self-esteem I have suggested that notices be placed in schools, churches, synagogues, and workplaces, inviting people to join in planning a self-fulfillment group. An announcement might read as follows:

BE ALL THAT YOU CAN BE
ANYONE INTERESTED IN SELF-FULFILLMENT?
SOME OF US ARE!
YOU MAY JOIN IN PLANNING A SELF-ENHANCEMENT
GROUP BY CALLING
JANE SMITH AT 444-1111
OR BILL SMITH AT 111-4444

You might also place notices on supermarket bulletin boards or in community newspapers. However, ads may attract curiosity seekers rather than people sincerely interested in self-help.

Responses to the notices may vary greatly. You may get many responses or few expressions of interest. Patience and perseverance are necessary when beginning. Keep in mind that Alcoholics Anonymous, which now numbers millions of people across the world, began with only two individuals who sought to help each other.

Just as individual and group therapy can complement each other, therapy groups and self-help groups can be mutually beneficial.

Some significant emotional changes may occur in self-help groups, but these occur spontaneously from the exchanges within the group rather than from issues analyzed professionally. For example, people who attend AA meetings may indeed have profound behavioral changes as they abstain from alcohol and begin to alter their addictive behavior. They may become less selfish, more considerate, more truthful, less cantankerous, and more forgiving as they examine their own behavior. However, these changes come about as gradual and spontaneous consequences of achieving sobriety, rather than from being analyzed and interpreted.

FIFTEEN

How It Worked for Barbara

It is extremely difficult to convey in writing how a group session works, whether it is a self-help or a therapy group. Many of the important transactions are nonverbal: gestures, facial expressions, other body language, vocal intonations, and so forth. Also, the changes generally occur gradually and extend over a long period of time. Reading an account of an effective group experience can result in the misconception that dramatic changes occur rapidly. Nothing could be farther from the truth.

Keep these two important points in mind when you read the case histories here. I will try to depict what happened to several people in groups. Remember that each example represents many sessions.

Barbara, twenty-nine, came to the group because she said she had a dilemma and needed advice, not therapy. Barbara enjoyed her work as a flight attendant, as well as a good salary. She lived with her widowed mother, her father having died at age fifty-two of a heart attack.

Barbara reported that her mother used to have an occasional drink, but after her father died, her mother's drinking increased. A year ago, when Barbara's younger brother went off to college, her mother's drinking increased to the point where she frequently became forgetful and occasionally stuporous. Barbara's flight schedule kept her away from home many days of the week. When Barbara began talking to her mother about the excessive drinking, she replied that she drank because she was lonely. She told Barbara that if she would quit her job with the airline, she would not drink so much. Barbara did not want to quit her job, but she felt guilty pursuing her own needs at the expense of neglecting her mother.

Two other people in the group were involved with conflicts over caregiving, and although their cases were different from Barbara's, there were enough similarities that they could provide support for her. Eventually it turned out that both these group members had feelings of unworthiness, and their caretaking bolstered their self-esteem.

Barbara had never thought of herself as having low self-esteem or that her concern for her mother was anything but the normal concern of a child for a parent. When her mother's drinking became symptomatic, Barbara had consulted an alcoholism specialist who told her that she was in no way responsible for her mother's drinking and not to allow her mother to convince her otherwise. She was told that quitting her job would not help her mother's alcohol problem. Nevertheless, Barbara continued to be in conflict, so she came to therapy. The group helped her realize that her inability to accept the recommendation of the professional indicated that there were other factors in her indecision.

After a number of sessions Barbara revealed for the first time that she had an older brother who had been a hellraiser since childhood. Both parents had been preoccupied with trying to control his behavior. In order to gain attention from her parents, Barbara became the "perfect child," trying to be different from her brother in every way. She made good grades at school, was helpful with the housework, prepared meals, and helped care for her younger brother. She had never realized that she harbored resentments against her parents for not showing enough appreciation for what she was doing, instead giving all the attention to the renegade brother, who eventually became addicted to drugs and drifted away.

Over a period of time Barbara was helped to see that her mother's loneliness was her mother's problem, and that as a healthy woman of fifty-six, she could do a lot to make her life interesting and enjoyable. Her mother did indeed need companionship, but as long as Barbara was available, her mother had no reason to look elsewhere. In other words, Barbara was not doing her mother a favor by staying with her. Her mother needed help to overcome her drinking problem and to establish herself in a relationship and perhaps a job. It became evident that Barbara wanted to stay with her mother to satisfy her own need to be loved. Since childhood she had been trying to earn her parents' love.

During the many sessions, Barbara was helped to see that she had many admirable qualities. The other group members genuinely cared for Barbara, and she was able to see that she could be liked by others even though she was not doing things for them. Barbara thus became aware that she was a person who deserved to be admired and loved in her own right. As she began to feel better about herself, she was able to see how her self-image had suffered in her childhood and how that had affected all other aspects of her life. She was having trouble developing meaningful relationships, and she had not taken advantage of promotional opportunities at work.

Eventually Barbara was able to extricate herself from the mother-job conflict. Together with her younger brother they had a therapeutic confrontation that resulted in her mother entering an alcoholism treatment program. Barbara's mother is now six years sober and has remarried. Barbara recently married and is working in a supervisory position with the airline.

Barbara's course in group therapy took about eighteen months with a group that met twice weekly. Although the presenting problem was indeed satisfactorily resolved, a number of other problems turned up, some of which she could not identify in herself but could easily see in other group members. The group helped her identify these problems in herself, too. As her self-image improved, she was able to overcome them as well.

SIXTEEN

How It Worked for Betty

At a public lecture, I spoke about the role of low self-esteem in eating disorders. I suggested that in addition to whatever therapy people were involved in, they should form small self-help groups to deal with problems of self-esteem. Following the lecture, eight people joined together to form a group. Three were anorexic-bulimics, three were compulsive overeaters, and two were family members of anorexic-bulimics (a husband and a mother). The family members were not related to others in the group.

Betty was the mother of a nineteen-year-old anorexic-bulimic. Her daughter was attending an out-of-town college and had refused treatment, so Betty joined the group to learn how to deal with her daughter. The group took a popular book on eating disorders as their text.

Betty was forty-five, and she had divorced her husband after fifteen years of emotional and physical abuse. Her daughter, Veronica, was the oldest of three children, with two younger brothers. Betty had recognized that her husband was abusive when she was pregnant with Veronica, but she did not turn to her parents for help because they had disapproved of the marriage and she wanted to show them that they were wrong. After the two boys were born, she began to see that she could not change her husband. She still wanted to turn to her parents for help, but she knew that they would tell her to leave her husband. She wanted to keep the marriage going for the children's sake; she was not going to allow them to suffer the problems of a broken home.

Things continued to deteriorate, and Betty got divorced when Veronica was eleven. Veronica did not react adversely to the divorce. She was a chubby child, but this did not appear to bother her. She did well in school and had friends. Veronica's eating disorder became apparent at age sixteen, when she took diet pills and starved herself to lose weight, but also had periodic binging. This continued until she left for college, and Betty was concerned that this erratic eating pattern would result in her flunking out.

After the first few sessions, someone in the group overheard Betty telling one of the bulimic young women that she would be happy to help her and to feel free to call her any time of the day or night, especially if she had the urge to binge. At the next session, the woman who had overheard the conversation raised the question of whether it was advisable for Betty to try to help this bulimic young woman. Her relationship with her own daughter had not helped the bulimia. Betty felt that she was being accused of having caused her daughter's bulimia and that the group assumed that she would exert a pathological effect on this woman. The group asked Betty why she had offered to make herself available any time of the day or night and wondered whether this wasn't putting herself out too much. Betty responded that when someone needed help immediately it would be a mistake to make her wait.

As far as Betty was concerned, the group emphasis gradually turned away from her daughter's bulimia to her own self-effacing behavior. Betty tended to apologize for things that did not require an apology. When anyone in the group said something critical of her, Betty would pout but would not defend her opinion.

At one point Betty shared that she was in a relationship with an abusive man. The group asked why she was allowing this relationship to continue, in light of her experience with her husband. Betty tried to justify the relationship, but the group was not convinced.

Eventually Betty let it be known that none of her three children really respected her and that they took advantage of her. She constantly did things for them but never demanded anything in return. The group pointed out that she had made a doormat of herself in her marriage, in her current relationship, and with her children.

The group helped Betty recognize that her behavior was caused by a poor self-image and showed her that they did not see her the way she saw herself. Betty presented very little information about her own personality development, and the group did not press her on it. Instead, she was encouraged to stand her ground with the man she was seeing and with her children.

The focus had shifted radically from what Betty could do for her daughter to what she could do for herself. In regard to her daughter, Betty came to realize that she was not responsible for Veronica's eating disorder and that she would accept help in time. Once Betty's self-image improved, she no longer needed to be the controlling mother and was able to accept that she was powerless over her daughter.

Don't assume that the group was preoccupied with Betty and her problems. (For demonstration purposes I focused on her.) As Betty made these favorable changes, so did other group members. The group was mutually supportive and shared in everyone's progress. When Betty stood her ground and refused to accept abuse from her gentleman friend, the group took pride in her achievement, just as Betty felt elated by the progress other group members made with their problems.

Again, this account is oversimplified. These weekly sessions went on for several years; it was a slow process. None of the changes occurred dramatically, and at times the group considered disbanding because they felt they were not accomplishing anything. On several occasions a professional group therapist was asked to evaluate the group and point them in a proper direction. After three years, the members concurred that they had achieved their goals, and the group dissolved, planning to meet every three months for old times' sake. There was general agreement that everyone had come to a more realistic and more positive self-awareness and that they were much more capable of coping with their respective problems. Those members who had been in larger groups, such as Overeaters Anonymous or Weight Watchers, felt that the small-group experience had not only enhanced their eating disorder recovery but had salutary effects in other aspects of their lives.

When one behavior change occurs, it can affect the entire personality. Personality is analogous to the decor of a room. If you buy a new chair, it may clash with the carpet, which now must be replaced. The old wallpaper now does not match the rugs, so that must be replaced. This necessitates new draperies that will blend with the wallpaper. By the time the changes have been completed, the room has a totally new look, which began with only a new chair.

Much the same happens with an alteration in personality. Change in any one character trait may throw the entire system out of harmony, and other traits may have to be altered. In this way, a totally new personality may eventually result.

A word of caution is necessary here. Although improvement in self-esteem is salutary, it may cause a disharmony in a relationship. For example, John and Mary seem to have a satisfactory marriage. A problem in Mary's life caused her to seek psychotherapy, and a negative self-image was diagnosed. Perhaps one of the manifestations of Mary's negative self-image was a passivity due to a lack of trust in her decision-making capabilities. As a consequence of this, Mary was very comfortable having her husband assume all the responsibilities of making decisions and perhaps controlling the family finances as well. John, on the other hand, likes to be in a controlling position, and Mary's passivity was exactly what he needed in a wife. If Mary's self-image changes so that she becomes more assertive and now wishes to participate in the decision making or have a say in the family finances, John may be displeased with the new development in her personality.

In other words, a relationship may begin with a nonverbalized understanding of the terms of the relationship. If either partner now significantly changes those terms, the basis for the relationship may disintegrate and an incompatibility develop.

This is why when someone has a problem with addiction, family members are also strongly urged to become involved in self-help groups. Otherwise, the recovering person may progress in personality development while the nonaddict spouse and/or children remain static. Similarly, it may be necessary for family members to make appropriate adjustments in themselves, and possibly even become involved in psychotherapy, when a close family member undergoes a self-image change.

SEVENTEEN

How It Worked for Linda

Linda sought treatment for alcohol and tranquilizer dependency at age thirty-four. Her use of alcohol began at age fifteen. Linda was very thin, probably anorexic, and her grandfather had suggested that she could gain weight by drinking beer because it is high in calories. Linda discovered that beer opened a new world for her. She had been very shy and self-conscious, avoiding relationships with boys and even with most girls. She did not think she could be liked.

Linda's father was a bookkeeper and her mother was a schoolteacher. She recalls them being very mechanical, providing a comfortable home but being emotionally detached. She had a twin brother who was very bright. Linda felt far inferior to him.

Once beer entered her system, Linda became a different person. She felt witty and sociable. She could relate well to boys, but she needed the alcohol to give her courage and bolster her personality. Although her reliance on beer kept increasing, it did not cause her any overt problems. She drank her way through college, where she majored in interior decorating. Upon graduation she got a job as a clothes buyer for a department store and occasionally did some furniture buying.

A few years later she fell in love with Alvin, an English instructor. Linda's parents did not approve of Alvin, but she married him anyway. Linda earned more than Alvin, who began relying on her income rather than his own. He became a substitute teacher and stayed home much of the time, claiming he was doing essential reading for his job, although he certainly did not advance himself in his profession. Alvin was markedly unhelpful in caring for the two children who were born in the first years of the marriage. He was constantly critical of Linda, who continued to work while trying to care for the children.

The quantity of alcohol Linda needed to keep her functioning could no longer be met by beer, and she switched to spirits. She found herself tremulous in the morning before her first drink but was concerned that the odor of whiskey would be detected at work. She obtained a prescription for Valium to get her through the day, turning to alcohol after work. She began to have memory lapses, which caused many problems at work and resulted in her losing her job. Soon after, Alvin sued for divorce and custody of the children, and Linda made a suicide attempt. When her alcohol and tranquilizer addictions were identified, she was referred to our rehabilitation center for treatment.

Linda's sense of unworthiness was understandable but unrealistic. She had considered herself inadequate even when she was supporting the family and running the household. Ridding herself of the unwarranted feelings of shame would be a major focus for her recovery. By realizing that her life had become unmanageable, she relinquished the illusion of needing to be a superperson and a supermom. She realized that it was okay to be just Linda, a human being who sometimes needed help.

Initially Linda was urged just to attend AA meetings and stay sober; psychodynamic insights could wait. She was fortunate in finding a sponsor with many years of sobriety who took a sincere interest in Linda and made herself available day and night for any of her problems.

After six months of sobriety, Linda found a part-time job as an interior decorator. She was able to get visitation rights to her children, who were happy to have their mother again. After the first year of sobriety, her sponsor suggested that she begin working on the fourth step, which was doing an inventory of her life.

Linda began to realize that she had suffered from unwarranted feelings of shame since childhood. She recalled how she had withdrawn from her friends and had isolated herself for no valid reasons. She now discovered that people enjoyed her company and that they actually sought her friendship.

One of the men she met in the recovery program became interested in Linda, who was thrilled to find that she could attract a man. Linda's sponsor was adamant that she not become sexually involved, pointing out that she was vulnerable to being sexually exploited because she was so starved for affection. Linda did avoid sexual entanglement and was pleasantly surprised to find that her friend was interested in her companionship even in the absence of sex.

Linda's employer was pleased with her work, and she began to work full time. She eventually did the fifth of the twelve steps in the AA program, sharing her history with an empathic priest who was able to help her see some of her self-image distortions.

After three years of sobriety, Linda was asked to become

a sponsor. Linda discovered in the woman she sponsored many of the self-image distortions and defense mechanisms that had been her own, and in helping her overcome these she was able to correct her own misperceptions. Linda was also able to see how her attraction to Alvin had been based on her erroneous self-concept. Her unwarranted feelings of shame and inadequacy had resulted in her becoming a doormat and tolerating his abuse.

As Linda progressed in her sobriety, her relationship with her children improved. They eventually expressed a desire to be with her rather than with their father, and Linda gladly assumed custody.

Linda excelled as an interior decorator and her boss offered her a partnership in the firm. Today Linda is nine years sober and has a very active social and business life, in addition to being the mother of two teenagers, hardly a small feat.

At a recent meeting, I asked Linda why she had not considered marriage. She laughed and said, "You've done too good a job on me. I now like myself so much that I don't think anyone else is good enough for me."

"You've restored my ego to the point where I now feel the need of a more prominent doctor"

Cartoon by Bill Hoest. Copyright Wm. Hoest Enterprises, Inc. Reprinted with permission.

EIGHTEEN

How It Worked for Adrienne, Ronald, and Amy

G roup therapy can be exciting. When a group of people get together with a sincere desire to improve their lives and overcome their emotional difficulties, anything can happen—and often does. Sometimes the group experience is intense and dramatic, as in the case of Adrienne.

Fifteen-year-old Adrienne had been referred to treatment by the juvenile detention center after she had been arrested for drinking and possession of marijuana.

In addition to marijuana and alcohol, Adrienne and her friends had used LSD, Percoset, Valium, and a variety of other substances that they got from their parents' medicine cabinets or on the street.

I asked Adrienne if she had ever worked in the kitchen and what she did with scraps of leftover food or peelings and the like. She said that she threw them in the garbage, of course. "Why don't you find someplace else to put them?" I asked. Adrienne responded that that was an absurd question, because there was no other place to throw garbage.

"Just look at this list of garbage you have used," I said.

"If you know garbage belongs in a garbage can, how come you put this in yourself?"

"I wanted to get high. All the kids were doing it."

"It is not quite true that all the kids were doing it. Some kids were doing it and some kids weren't, and you chose to associate with those who did. My guess is that you thought of yourself as being some kind of garbage can, and that's why you put this garbage in yourself."

Adrienne's eyes became a bit misty. "I never thought I was any good," she said.

Adrienne's mother was sixteen when Adrienne was born. Another child was born two years later. When Adrienne was four, her alcoholic father disappeared. Her mother was overwhelmed with the care of two children without financial or emotional support and had them placed in foster homes.

Adrienne began acting out against authority at an early age, and she did poorly in school. She was more than her foster parents could manage, and it was evident to Adrienne that they were not thrilled to have her. To Adrienne the world was a hostile place, where you get what you fight for, and the weaker ones lose out.

Adrienne appeared to be a very sweet, lovable, and sensitive young woman who was full of anger at being dealt a raw deal. Her defiance against authority and refusal to comply with rules became apparent in the therapy group. The therapist tried desperately to reach her and invested much time and effort in individual sessions, making only a slight dent in her armor. It seemed as though Adrienne was trying to get herself kicked out, perhaps because she had come to expect rejection as normal in life.

During the third week of therapy, Adrienne announced that she was leaving treatment. The therapist told her that she would be returned to the juvenile detention center if she left against the staff's advice. Adrienne did not care; she would leave anyway. The group tried to convince her how foolish this would be, but she would not budge.

At this point the therapist broke down crying and left the room. After several minutes the therapist returned, still tearful, accompanied by a staff member. She said that she was going to quit because she could not tolerate investing so much of herself in another person and seeing her self-destruct. "I put everything I had into Adrienne because I feel for her and know that she can make it. My father abandoned us when we were little, and I know what she feels like, but that's no reason to destroy herself."

Adrienne got up and sat near the therapist, putting her arms around her, and both cried together. The role reversal was striking. Several of the group cried along with them. The first one to speak was Adrienne, who said, "I'm sorry to hurt you, and I appreciate your caring, but my mind is made up. I'm going to leave and take my chances." The group tried to persuade Adrienne to stay, but to no avail. There was much shouting at her, but she just shouted back.

The following morning Adrienne requested a session with the staff supervisor and confided that she had been taken by surprise. She couldn't remember anyone ever caring for her before. "I was an imposition on everybody. I was a piece of crap that no one could get rid of. Yesterday was the first time in my life somebody really cared about what was going to happen to me. I don't know how to handle that yet. I'm so confused. I want to stay just a few days more to figure things out."

This incident was not planned or orchestrated; it was a spontaneous occurrence in an empathic setting. These are the kinds of things that can occur in such an environment.

Adrienne's story does have a happy ending. She completed residential treatment, and arrangements were made with an appropriate foster family, who was supportive during the next two years of outpatient treatment. She graduated from high school with good grades and went to community college. She is considering a course in counseling, hoping to put her personal experience to work.

Ronald is a young man of eighteen who had a group experience of another kind. Prior to admission to our facility he had been living on the street. His self-concept can be summed up by two statements in his self-evaluation sheet. In response to what he thinks of himself, he wrote, "A worthless piece of shit," and in response to a question about what he feels most positive about, he wrote, "I can beat up my older brother."

In a group discussion, Ronald said that he began using alcohol and drugs when he was eleven. His only drug-free period lasted for eight months when he lived with his grandmother who was disabled by a stroke. He had cooked, kept house, done the shopping, and looked after her until she died. The therapist asked why he had not listed this as one of his accomplishments, but Ronald dismissed the question as insignificant.

One of the group members picked up on this point and said that it was too important to dismiss. It was obvious that when Ronald was doing something worthwhile, he was able to abstain from drugs. With the help of the therapist, the group focused on Ronald's inability to accept his achievements, particularly the caring aspect of his personality. This served as a wedge to pry open the tight seal of self-denigration. This single item helped Ronald realize that he had been unable to accept anything positive about himself and served as the seedling of self-esteem that was expanded in therapy.

Amy, age sixteen, also presented a thoroughly worthless image of herself. She said that she had abandoned herself to a life of drugs and prostitution and didn't really care what happened to her.

One of the group shrewdly commented, "If you don't care at all about yourself, why are you wearing braces? Obviously, you do care about yourself, at least about your appearance."

Amy denied this and said that the aunt she lived with had a daughter about her age who had braces. Her uncle and aunt felt that if they did not provide Amy with equal treatment, they would be showing favoritism. "They don't care about how I look either. It's just that my aunt feels guilty about my being an orphan, and she does things for me for the sake of my mother."

The group did not accept this. "Wearing braces is no fun, and if you didn't want them you could have said no. The fact that you are wearing them shows that you do care about yourself. All the stuff you are giving us about not giving a damn about yourself is just a big lie."

Amy's facade of self-abandonment was gently and successfully dismantled by the group. She was eventually helped to see that she cared very much about herself but had despaired of anyone else caring for her.

Although insights such as these can be brought out in individual therapy, the variety of experiences and the impact that peers can exert greatly increase the efficacy of treatment in a group. It matters little what the presenting symptom is. The underlying factor of a negative self-image invariably emerges and can be more easily corrected in a group setting.

Part IV

Dealing with Problems Along the Way

NINETEEN

Relapse versus Growth

R ecovery from a negative self-image is gradual. As is the case with any extended recovery process, the course is not a steadily smooth uphill slope. One does eventually reach the top, but rarely without sustaining some slips on the way.

Slips that occur after a person has begun to improve may be more painful than the original chronic depressive state. It's like falling off a ladder. If you are standing on the first rung, the fall probably won't cause any injury. The higher you have climbed on the ladder, the more severe the fall. Similarly, someone who has felt more or less unhappy day after day may actually have become accustomed to that state of existence. If the person begins to feel much better and then has a recurrence of even a brief depression, this is felt much more keenly.

Even after reaching an essentially stable stage, there is always the possibility of relapse. To understand why this happens, try a simple exercise. Take a piece of thick cardboard and fold one corner. Now straighten out the fold. Where the cardboard was folded, there is a crease. This crease will remain regardless of how much you flatten the fold. If you try to bend the cardboard at any other place, you will encounter some resistance, but at the crease, the slightest pressure makes the cardboard bend.

A person who recovers from a negative self-image may be left with a "crease." Anything that occurs, even years later, that constitutes a threat to the ego is likely to resurrect all the feelings of inadequacy that he or she had already overcome. Some or all of the symptoms that accompanied the negative self-image may emerge again. People who have recovered from alcoholism or another chemical dependency are vulnerable to relapse into chemical use at this time. Awareness of this possibility may help prevent a panic reaction or chemical use in the event of a relapse.

Subsequent challenges to the ego are highly probable. If we continue to function at a fixed low level of performance we do not arouse any expectations from anyone. We, our families, and our employers won't expect more of us than our routine performance. As we gain self-confidence, our performance level is likely to increase, and as a consequence we may be given additional assignments. Our employers may assign us to new duties, our families may expect more, and we ourselves may accept new challenges. Just as the cardboard yields with even minimal pressure, any new expectation of us may constitute a stress, which can reawaken the feelings of inadequacy that had been lying dormant.

Earlier I reported the case of a physician who had achieved outstanding scholastic honors yet had a very poor self-image. Her alcoholism had resulted in her dismissal as medical director of a health facility.

Early in her recovery she took a part-time job with relatively minimal responsibilities. After several weeks, she encountered some very severe stresses. I suggested that she discuss this with her AA sponsor. Several weeks later she again reported being in a crisis, and I gave her the same advice. I inquired how the previous crisis had been resolved, and she stated that it had been trivial, but this time she was really in a severe crisis.

These calls recurred every few weeks with an identical pattern. What had been a major crisis several weeks earlier had been easily resolved, but this time it was major.

In a therapeutic interview I pointed out this pattern to the physician. As she performed successfully at work, new demands were constantly being made of her. No one asks someone who is functioning poorly to do more, but people who perform well are very likely to be asked to increase their functioning. Each new demand resurrected her self-doubts and constituted a crisis. With the help of her sponsor, each hurdle was overcome, allowing her to function at a higher level, which then led to increased expectations of her, resulting in a very positive but stressful cycle.

The same stresses that may trigger a relapse may also be stimuli for growth. I once came across a fascinating description of how lobsters grow. The lobster, encased in a hard, unyielding shell, grows until the shell becomes restrictive and stifling. It then retreats to a sheltered place, sheds its shell, and gradually forms a new one. This process is repeated numerous times until the lobster reaches its maximum size. Each time the lobster sheds its shell, even in the safety of its retreat, it is at the mercy of sudden currents of water or predatory fish. The outer shell is its protective armor, and when it temporarily loses this defense it become vulnerable. Yet in order to grow, the lobster must take such risks.

I have often told lobster lovers that they should be grateful that lobsters do not have recourse to doctors. If they did, then at the first sign of discomfort, the lobster would get a prescription for a tranquilizer. Instead of shedding its shell and growing, it would eliminate its discomfort with medication and would remain in its tiny original shell until it died.

When you feel emotionally uncomfortable, think of this as a possible signal that you are ready for a growth spurt. You may indeed get relief from a chemical, but it will stifle further growth. If you present your problem to a counselor, therapist, sponsor, or someone who can help put things in their proper perspective, a relapse can be averted and actual growth may occur. People who maintain contact with a self-help group have an accessible resource that can prevent a psychological relapse from escalating into a full-blown negative self-image problem again, or into recourse to chemical use.

TWENTY

Resistance to Self-Awareness

Many people with a negative self-image exhibit a reluctance to discover their true selves. They are convinced that a self-discovery will reveal only the negative aspects of their personality. Confronting these goblins is indeed frightening.

We all have things in the past of which we are not proud. But these should not deter us from self-discovery. We should talk about them, learn from them, and then discard them.

Sometimes resistance to self-exploration does not come from fear of discovering character defects. The people I mentioned earlier who have a fear of happiness are reluctant to discover their virtues and personality assets.

To understand why someone wouldn't want to discover her assets, consider Pat. This twenty-three-year-old woman was admitted to treatment for a drinking problem. At the admission interview, she asked whether she could undergo psychological testing.

"Why do you want psychological tests?" I asked.

"I'm afraid I might have brain damage from drinking," she said.

I assured her that she did not have any brain damage and that there was no need for psychological tests. However, the following day she inquired whether she might have a brain-wave test, and I again assured her that there was no need. The next day she requested a CT scan of the brain.

"I have already told you that you do not have brain damage," I said.

"But how can you be sure? You don't know how much I drank."

Pat's inability to accept reassurance puzzled me, but after a lengthy interview the mystery was solved. She *wanted* to have brain damage! Then she could say to her family, "Leave me alone. I am not capable of achieving sobriety. Recovery from alcoholism is difficult enough for normal people, but I am brain damaged and cannot be expected to overcome my addiction." Similarly, if they wanted her to become gainfully employed, she could say, "Me? Hold a job? You must be kidding. I can't take on any responsibility. I'm brain damaged." If she was urged to go to school, she would say, "Me? College? Impossible. I'm brain damaged." As tragic as brain damage is, it would have been the perfect out, exempting her from any efforts to remain sober and improve her life.

Variations of this attitude can be discovered in many people. There is a strange kind of comfort in resigning ourselves to a state of inadequacy. We are then exempt from trying.

Again, participants in a group effort can diminish this resistance in two ways. First, it's likely that a person harboring such resistance will observe it in another person and can then be helped to discover it in himself or herself. Second, the encouragement and support of the group can help overcome the anxiety resulting from the implied need to perform at a higher level and assume greater responsibilities.

Ethan complained in his therapy group that his work performance had recently deteriorated, and he attributed this to anxiety he felt over an impending promotion. He was about to be elevated to a supervisory position, and he questioned his capacity to give direction to others. His worries about disappointing everyone and failing in this new position were interfering with his concentration. One group member suggested that perhaps his diminished performance was his way of persuading his superiors that he was not as capable as they thought he was and that they should retract the promotion.

Another group member was a retired executive who offered to provide Ethan with some guidance in a supervisory role. In fact, this person was bored in his retirement and welcomed the opportunity to share his experience with Ethan. Ethan did accept the promotion and performed very well in his new position. The therapist then raised the question of whether there might not be other instances in which Ethan performed inadequately in order to avoid being asked to take on greater responsibilities. It emerged that this had indeed been a pervasive trait in Ethan's life, which had affected his domestic and social, as well as occupational, life.

Pinpointing this single self-defeating tactic helped Ethan investigate other ways he was avoiding responsibilities that would promote positive feelings about himself.

TWENTY-ONE

Getting in Touch with Feelings

A true awareness of the self, the whole self, requires an awareness of all our feelings. Frequently, we disown some feelings because we consider them improper, because we are afraid we cannot control them, or because they are simply too painful. There may be considerable resistance to acknowledging these feelings, and as long as we continue to disown them, we cannot arrive at a valid self-awareness.

It is easy to understand why some feelings are disowned. What is harder to understand is why it is difficult to acknowledge perfectly normal, positive, and even salutary feelings. I gained some insight into this phenomenon as a result of two events that followed in close succession, one at home and the other at work.

One day my wife pointed out to me that the faucet on the laundry tub was leaking. When I tried to turn the valve to cut off the water flow to the faucet, I was unable to do so and had to call a plumber. The plumber was no more successful at this than I was, and he explained that the valve was frozen in its position and had probably not been touched since the house had been built seventy years earlier. The only way to fix the faucet was to turn off the main valve that controlled water flow to the entire house.

After the water was shut off and the faucet dismantled, the plumber confronted me with the sad findings that the entire interior of the faucet was eroded, and the unit had to be replaced. After the work was finished and the main water valve was turned on, I discovered that every time I turned on any faucet in the house there was an initial explosive discharge of rusty water, which gradually became a smooth, clear flow.

The following day I saw a young man in consultation. After two weeks of intensive group therapy, Joshua appeared to be detached from all feelings, showing no emotion whatever. During the interview it emerged that when he was ten, his father died suddenly, and he recalled looking at himself at the mirror and saying, "You are not going to cry," and indeed he did not.

It became evident that at age ten Joshua had tried to shield himself from feeling grief, but because he was unable to find a way to turn off this specific feeling, he turned off the "main valve," as it were, shutting off *all* feelings. Not only did he not experience the pain of grief, but he had rendered himself insensitive to all emotions, sad as well as happy. Since age ten he had felt no anger, no pride, no love, no joy.

The problem he now confronted was that in order to experience feelings, *any* feelings, he had to open the "main valve." Having been without feelings of any kind for so long, he saw this as threatening. He felt that emotions of any kind would overwhelm him, much as the opening of any faucet after the main valve was turned on was followed by an explosive discharge. He therefore was frightened of joy and pride as well as shame and sadness.

Once Joshua understood this, he allowed himself to relax his guard a bit. His group provided the support necessary to carry him through the initial experience of feeling emotions once again. It is much easier to understand why someone would wish to avoid painful feelings, and indeed it is quite common to utilize one or more psychological defense mechanisms to protect us from emotional distress. There are times, however, especially in therapy, when we should recognize the experience of emotional distress as a positive, growth phenomenon.

At our rehabilitation center one day, a young man asked to speak to me privately, then threw his arms around my neck and began crying bitterly. "You've got to help me, Doc," he sobbed. "I can't take it. I can't take the pain." He told me he had entered our facility the day before. Paul was twenty-three and had been using drugs since he was fourteen.

"From the time that you began using until now, what was your longest period of abstinence?" I asked.

"I haven't had any," Paul answered.

I then told him about a young woman who had been involved in a serious automobile accident, sustaining multiple fractures. She had no sensation or motion in her right arm. The neurosurgeon performed a nerve repair but explained to her that there was no guarantee that feeling would recur. It would be perhaps three to four months before the success of the operation could be determined.

After three months had passed, she dropped a lit cigarette she was holding in her left hand, and it fell on her right hand, causing her to feel pain. She promptly jumped up in joy and ran around the room happily screaming, "I'm hurting! I felt pain!"

For this woman, the pain was an indication that the surgery had been successful. The distress of the burn paled in significance to the tidings it bore, that she would have the use of her right hand again.

I then pointed out to Paul that for nine years he had essentially anesthetized his brain with chemicals and had felt no sensations whatever, neither joy nor sadness. Paralyzing the brain with drugs had arrested his personality development. Now that the drugs were out of his system, his capacity to feel was returning, and this meant that he would be able to grow and mature. Although I empathized with his suffering, I stressed that the positive aspect of being able to feel again should outweigh his pain. "What you ought to do," I said, "is to go into the lobby and shout for joy, 'I'm depressed! I'm depressed!' just as the woman danced for joy to feel pain. You are regaining the function of your mind, and that should be a euphoric experience, in spite of the distress."

Chemicals are not the only method people use to avoid feelings. Our unconscious mind may shield us from distress, and it may take considerable effort to overcome these natural protective maneuvers. However, no true self-awareness can be achieved as long as we alienate a part of the self from the whole.

TWENTY-TWO

Anger and Hostility

From the writings of Sigmund Freud, it is apparent that in his days repressed sexuality was a major psychological problem. In these days there is very little about sexuality that is repressed. Instead, the prime emotional culprit today is probably repressed anger.

Many of us have difficulty with anger. We are taught in early life that feeling angry is wrong. As children we are scolded when we express anger. Some of us fear that expressing anger will prevent people from loving us. In whatever way it comes about, there is a widespread impression that it is bad to express anger or to be hateful. Consequently, people who do harbor such feelings are apt to think of themselves as bad or unworthy, and this contributes to feelings of shame that may have their onset very early in life.

Let me define my terms. Anger is a feeling that is aroused when we are provoked, either physically or by being denied something we desire and believe is rightfully ours, or by an insult to our pride. The feeling that results from such provocation is beyond our control. In other words, we cannot choose not to be angry when provoked. The most we can do is to repress the anger, which may occur if we are convinced that feeling angry is wrong or a threat to our likability. Repressed anger is pushed into the unconscious portion of the mind where it is beyond reach and cannot be properly dissipated. It slowly festers and exerts damaging effects on other feelings and behavior.

If anger is what we feel when we are provoked, and we realize that we have no voluntary control over this emotional response, then we can avoid thinking of ourselves as bad for allowing such feelings to occur. Anger is not a matter of choice. Furthermore, such anger will occur even if the person who provokes us is someone we love, including parents, spouse, children, friends, or God. To sum it up: It is not wrong or sinful to feel anger.

What we do with the feeling of anger is something altogether different, because we have choices on how to manage the feeling. Repressing anger can result in emotional upset, and some psychologists advocate discharging the anger by screaming or hitting a punching bag. There is not a shred of evidence that this diminishes anger; to the contrary, it may intensify anger.

One of the most important things to know about anger is that although we may be unable to prevent it, we are capable of controlling its expression. Many people fear that they will not be able to control their anger and will lose the affection of loved ones who are the targets of their anger. This is like having a minefield within oneself and being under the constant tension of "what will happen if I explode." We should develop confidence in our ability to control our behavior and realize that although we may have no control over some *feelings,* we have a great deal of control over our *actions.*

If the fear of anger is eliminated, we can begin safely to dissipate it, not by kicking the cat or hitting the wall, but by simple reflection. First, were we correct in assessing the provocation? Sometimes the provocation is unintentional—someone steps on our toes in the theater or even accidentally spills coffee on us. There is a momentary flash of anger, which soon passes after the person says "I'm sorry." We have all been perpetrators of such accidents, and because we can easily understand that there was no malice, our anger quickly dissolves. But note: Even in such common situations, anger does occur, because it is an involuntary reflex response. It is brief because we can easily empathize and dismiss it. This is the prototype of a reasonable response to anger: Feel it and then dismiss it.

This is not as easily achieved when the injury or insult is more severe and where there was indeed malice. The feeling of anger is more intense, and there is invariably an impulse to retaliate. Even if we try to comply with a spiritual requirement to forgive, the anger remains.

In working with alcoholics, I have witnessed a useful technique. A recovering corporate attorney found himself suddenly unemployed as a result of company downsizing. Not having been in private practice and not having saved any money during his years of active drinking, he was in dire straits. He was then approached by a group of investors who wished to develop a chain of retail outlets, and they made him president of the new venture. Once he had opened three stores for them, they voted to oust him, and it was evident that they had simply exploited him. I met him shortly after his ouster and he said, "I am very bitter about this, but I will go to an AA meeting tonight and drop off my resentments there. You see, if I hang on to them, I will drink again, and that is something I refuse to do."

This man realized the destructiveness of harboring resentments. In his situation the danger was clear: relapse into drinking. The awareness of this danger led him to seek ways to dispose of his resentments. Hanging on to them would not achieve anything for him and could seriously aggravate his plight.

People who are not concerned about a relapse into drinking may not be aware that there are other harmful effects in harboring resentments. The internal rage may cause or contribute to depression or to many psychosomatic conditions such as migraine, high blood pressure, or ulcers. Simply for survival purposes, we must find a way to dissipate anger.

How does involvement in AA or other self-help group relieve resentments? You ventilate your feelings to sympathetic ears. Others may respond with similar experiences of their own, and sincere empathy can provide much relief. Some may point out that what they had seen as unqualified disasters subsequently turned out to be blessings in disguise. Sometimes an objective observer may point out that your interpretation of the incident was mistaken, and you can achieve a perspective that significantly mitigates the episode. Finally, you can be helped to realize that we do foolish things that harm others and later regret them. Perhaps those who harmed us regretted their actions.

The attorney did indeed benefit from AA meetings. He is now the chief executive officer of a billion-dollar corporation and in a much stronger position than had he continued with the retail outlet venture. He now looks at that unpleasant episode as a blessing in disguise.

Since anger and hostility are intimately associated with early feelings of shame, their continued existence, even if justified, is likely to rekindle or perpetuate feelings of shame. We do not have to be motivated to achieve sainthood in order to rid ourselves of anger. It is simply in the best interest of our physical and emotional health.

TWENTY-THREE

Shame versus Guilt

S hame and guilt are both unpleasant emotions. They are often used interchangeably, and a person may say "I feel guilty for what I've done" and "I'm ashamed of what I did," referring to the same act. Actually these two easily confused feelings are different, and it is helpful to distinguish between them.

According to current psychological thinking, guilt comes from doing something wrong, violating a moral or ethical principle. When such a violation occurs, guilt is a healthy feeling. It stimulates us to rectify the wrong by making restitution, by apologizing, or by religious expiation, whichever is appropriate. The discomfort of guilt also serves a preventative purpose. It can discourage us from wrongdoing because of the knowledge that afterward we will feel guilty.

There is also an unhealthy type of guilt, which occurs when we feel guilty for something that was not a violation of a moral or ethical principle. Pathologic guilt may occur when we only fantasize a misdeed. We may also feel guilty for harboring an improper thought, even though we aren't

"Thank goodness for guilt!"

Grin & Bear It by Wagner. Reprinted with special permission of North American Syndicate.

able to control the thought. In such cases, making amends or expiating is of no value because there is no realistic basis for guilt. This type of guilt requires psychological treatment.

I recall Sally, whose father died of a heart attack when she was twelve. She came into treatment at age thirty-eight, consumed with guilt because she felt she was responsible for her father's death. She confessed this "sin" numerous times, and finally a priest recommended psychiatric counseling. He understood that she was not confessing a real sin and that her feeling guilty for her father's death was inappropriate. This is an example of unhealthy guilt.

However, whether the guilt is healthy or unhealthy, both are related to an act, real or fantasized. Guilt is thus the feeling accompanying "I made a mistake."

Shame is of a different character and may have nothing to do with a real or fantasized act. Shame is a feeling of "I am no good." If an automobile that was functioning perfectly could think and feel, and had the feeling of "I am a lemon," that would be equivalent to shame. In such a case, there is no way to fix the car, since there is nothing wrong with it. If guilt can be summed up as "I *made* a mistake," shame is the feeling "I *am* a mistake," when there is no justification in reality for such a feeling.

Shame is a deeper, more painful, and more pervasive feeling than guilt. Whereas we can relieve guilt through amends or expiation, there is no similar action that can remove the feeling of shame. Thus, shame may result in despair.

Humans are complex organisms. Our bodies are kept healthy by a host of automatic defensive and internal control mechanisms that operate beyond our awareness. The immune system, the white blood cells, the hormone levels, and sundry other systems respond to changes in the environment to protect and preserve us.

This is also true of the psychological system. The unconscious mind utilizes a number of mechanisms to protect our ego.

As I have noted, the feeling of shame is essentially hopeless. If I am essentially bad, regardless of my behavior I am doomed. If my very essence is unlikable, then I will never be likable, because my essence cannot change. I am therefore doomed to a life of loneliness and rejection.

This feeling is so intolerable that the unconscious mind sets into operation one of its ingenious mechanisms to help us feel better. If the unconscious could speak aloud, we would hear it say, "I can help you get rid of this torment of feeling doomed to eternal unlikability. Here's what you do: Provoke people to dislike you. Be rude and obnoxious. Then when people don't like you, you can attribute it to your behavior rather than to your essence. You will have the comfort of thinking, 'I really am basically a likable person, and people would like me and will like me when I stop my obnoxious behavior.' But if you don't behave obnoxiously, you will have to attribute your being disliked to your very essence, and that is an unbearable pain, because there is no relief."

Harry Stack Sullivan, one of America's greatest psychiatrists, said, "It is easier for a person to feel rejected for what one *does* than for what one *is*." This was echoed by a recovering alcoholic and drug addict, who by age thirty-two had spent more than half his life in reformatories, prisons, and mental hospitals. In a talk he gave at an AA meeting, he mused, "Why did I drink and use drugs? I don't know." Then he paused and said, "Yeah, I do know why. I wanted people to hate me because I was a drunk and a junkie, not because I was Richie."

This is a keen insight. Richie was convinced that people would dislike him, and he had felt this way since childhood. To think he was despised because he was Richie was intolerable because he had no way of being anyone but Richie. If, however, he could attribute people's despising him to his obnoxious behavior, this was much less painful. He could console himself with the thought that he could become likable if he just stopped provoking people. In this way, he would not have to think himself doomed to loneliness.

Nancy by Jerry Scott. Reprinted by permission of United Feature Syndicate, Inc.

This defense mechanism is widespread. Because it rests on a false assumption, it is both tragic and destructive. Richie was in fact a likable person. People who are likable, and who could enjoy companionship and intimacy, may resign themselves to a life of solitude. Richie suffered from delusions of inadequacy, unworthiness, and unlikability—in a word, shame. What the unconscious does in some cases is to convert shame to guilt. Unfortunately, as long as this unwarranted shame persists, its conversion to guilt continues, and the provocative behavior persists.

Unless the underlying shame is eliminated, it is impossible to eliminate destructive behavior. This may be one of the factors in recidivism, where people repeat antisocial acts and are not deterred by the prospects of imprisonment. They are convinced that they will be ostracized regardless of what they do, and their antisocial behavior makes the inevitable ostracism more tolerable. Richie and many others like him can attest to this. Richie's change of behavior followed a therapeutic breakthrough in which he was able, perhaps for the first time in his life, to feel that he was likable.

As I mentioned, people who suffer from shame may have difficulty accepting good things and often anticipate distress. The woman in Chapter 1 is an example of this. Because of the abscesses that resulted from her heavy drug use, she had to be hospitalized for two weeks and then returned for rehabilitation. Two weeks into the latter, I met her in the lobby and was impressed by her physical improvement. She had been free of drugs for four weeks, was receiving proper nutrition, and her infections had cleared up. I remarked to her, "You're really looking good."

I was stunned when my innocent remark evoked a response of expletives. The following day she apologized:

"I'm sorry for what I said yesterday. You said something positive to me, and I just don't know how to handle that."

People who are shame-ridden may actually feel more comfortable when they are treated poorly, since this is familiar to them. Salutary treatment may constitute a challenge they do not know how to manage. In this way shame may be self-perpetuating, since their behavior is likely to elicit reactions that confirm their low self-worth.

TWENTY-FOUR

Learning Our Limitations

Healthy self-esteem is the result of valid self-assessment, neither underestimating nor overestimating oneself. Indeed, overestimation that is manifested as grandiosity is invariably a defense against feelings of unworthiness. People who feel adequate and worthy do not need to boast about their importance, and they do not need the accolades of others to give them a feeling of worth.

Realizing our limitations is no reason for feeling inadequate. Adequacy depends on what we are supposed to do. The fact that a harmonica cannot produce the music of an accordion does not detract from its excellence as a harmonica. We need to be aware of our limitations, but this should not cause us to feel deficient. People with low self-esteem often see normal limitations as defects and try to be superhuman.

Eek & Meek® by Howie Schneider. Reprinted by permission of Newspaper Enterprise Association, Inc.

Meek is right. Our limitations are a fact of life. Others recognize them in us. Why should we deny them?

A classic example of denying limitations is the alcoholic. Alcoholism deprives a person of self-control. There is increasing evidence that this loss of control is biochemical and has nothing to do with willpower. People who are strong in every other personality trait may lack control in regard to alcohol. This lack of control is a natural limitation, similar to the lack of control of the hay fever sufferer who inhales pollen. However, alcoholics classically refuse to accept their natural limitations and deny that they have a disease. They consider control of alcohol to be totally volitional and view the absence of control as a defect. They cannot admit to having such a defect.

We are not omnipotent. An accurate assessment of human capabilities reveals many limitations. If we think we should not have certain limitations, we may consider ourselves deficient, and this may result in feelings of shame. Insisting that we should be what we cannot be constitutes false pride, which is often a defensive response to shame.

False pride is frequently evident in regard to accepting help. Because of normal limitations and frailties, we are often in need of help. Some people reject help, seeing its acceptance as an indication of weakness. Indeed, they may see dependence of any kind as a weakness and exhibit independence even to their own detriment. It is not unusual to see a person like this who has suffered a heart attack disconnect the intravenous tubes and monitors in the intensive care unit and leave the hospital against medical advice. Some people engage in dangerous, reckless behavior, as though they were not subject to human vulnerabilities.

On the other hand, awareness of our true potential should result in both true pride and humility: pride in our capacity for excellence, and humility in the realization that given our enormous capacities, we have hardly scratched the surface in terms of achievement. True pride and humility both militate against self-destructive behavior of any kind. We realize that we are too valuable to damage and that self-destructive behavior will diminish our capacity to achieve.

A thorough self-analysis should result in awareness of our capacity to achieve, which should stimulate us to greater performance and acceptance of our limitations.

People can be motivated to perform by two forces, one healthy and the other unhealthy. To the casual observer, both may seem to be doing the same thing, but they are as different as night is from day. There is a distinction between high achievers and overachievers.

High achievers are gifted and know that they have something to offer. They have positive feelings about themselves and enjoy sharing themselves with others. The more they give, the more they are stimulated to give. As a result, they may never reach an end point because they are always stimulated to do more. However, the need to do more does not detract from the satisfaction of what has already been done.

The prototype for the high achiever is a nursing mother. She may be uncomfortable when her breasts are engorged with milk and feel great relief when her infant nurses. However, in several hours her milk supply is replenished, and she again experiences discomfort until the baby again nurses. The repeated discomfort does not diminish the feeling of satisfaction of having fed the baby earlier.

We can probably all recall having instructors who enjoyed teaching and who were stimulated when students challenged them to produce more. We may have observed artists who love to perform and cheerfully respond to requests for encores and enjoy giving them perhaps even more than the audience enjoys listening to them.

High achievers may never be able to sit back and do nothing for long periods of time. Yet they can relax at intervals, having enjoyed their past performances.

Overachievers may be equally gifted, but they operate out of shame. A gnawing sensation that they are somehow not good drives them to vindicate themselves by performance. They may indeed achieve great things, but even realization of the achievements does not give them lasting relief. The reason for this is that we can never successfully compensate for a deficiency that does not in fact exist. Real deficiencies can be compensated for, as when a blind person develops an acute sense of touch or hearing. But if a person who is very attractive has the delusion that he is homely, nothing that he does will eliminate that feeling of homeliness. Overachievers, by definition, desperately try to gain a feeling of worth to assuage the pain of feeling unworthy. Since their feelings are unwarranted, nothing they do is likely to eliminate the feeling of shame. Overachievers may have a momentary feeling of worth when their achievements are publicly acknowledged, but within seconds the feeling of being not good enough overtakes them.

Like high achievers, overachievers always do more and

more but, in sharp contrast to high achievers, are never satisfied. They cannot relax because they are shame-conscious. Consequently, they may eschew relaxation and constantly push themselves. As we have seen, shame-oriented people may not accept realistic limitations, and overachievers may overexert themselves. Overachievers are therefore more vulnerable to diseases of stress such as high blood pressure, heart attacks, ulcers, and migraines.

I was asked to see a patient in consultation because of a recurrent bleeding peptic ulcer. Tom was in his forties, a very ambitious man who had become wealthy as a result of his business endeavors. He was constantly on the go, and in addition to his many business commitments was in the forefront of community activities. He had received wide acclaim for his contributions.

"If you walk into my living room," Tom said, "you will see a wall full of plaques and tributes. They mean nothing to me." Although he had done much good, which he should have enjoyed, his motivation was to prove himself, something he could never successfully accomplish.

Overcoming a negative self-concept allows overachievers to become high achievers. The goal of changing the self-concept to a positive one is not to convert an ambitious person into a beachcomber, but to allow the person to perform at the same high level without jeopardizing his or her physical and emotional health.

Just as it is appropriate to tell an alcoholic or drug addict, "You're too good to do this to yourself," it is appropriate to say this to an overachiever. An awareness of one's positivity will allow a person to achieve without inflicting damage on himself or herself.

TWENTY-FIVE

Setting Priorities

We must decide on the role or roles we desire for ourselves. Too often we drift through life rather than steer a course. Defining a role at least enables us to steer. Drifting may result in letting others define our role.

What is it that I wish to be? If I wish to have several roles, is this realistic, or must I relinquish one or more? If I desire to maintain several roles, which takes priority?

A woman may decide that she wishes to be a wife, mother, daughter, professional person, and active community member. Looking back on her pattern of functioning, she may find that the demands of all these roles have on occasion caused conflict. When a particular function could not be fulfilled, she may have considered herself to have failed in that role. Reevaluating herself in the light of realistic goals will allow her to set priorities and to realize that making a choice between conflicting demands on her time and energies does not constitute dereliction.

Clear definition and prioritization can result in a more efficient modus operandi. For example, it may be possible to maintain multiple roles if we delegate certain functions.

We must decide which functions we wish to delegate and which we wish to fulfill personally. Then delegation can be accomplished without inappropriate guilt.

Some working people feel guilty that they put their small children in day care or that an older child is a latchkey child, coming home from school to an empty home. They may feel that they are derelict in proper parenting. This is a typical area of parent-career conflict and may cause emotional distress.

Resolution of the conflict does not mean abandoning either role. Choosing a proper day-care program and spending quality time with children may permit very wholesome parenting. If the career absorbs so much time and energy that it encroaches on adequate relationships with the children, we can delegate some career responsibilities or even cut back. When done with proper planning and consistency, neither function need suffer. Problems arise when we move helter-skelter, investing more time at home one week, perhaps driven by guilt, and more time at the office the next week, being spurred on by ambition or professional demands. This inconsistency can result in confusion and a great deal of emotional turmoil.

Ventilating these conflicts in a group and receiving objective input may allow a parent to arrive at a plan for living, as well as to make midcourse changes when they are called for. A child's illness or any other crisis at home may cause chaos in a person who is drifting, but can be managed much more efficiently if one is steering.

Ellen came to one session of her self-help group very upset. She had advanced to a supervisory position in her company and was under particular stress because labor problems at the firm had resulted in a much greater workload for her. Several weeks earlier her father had suffered a stroke and was now to be discharged from the hospital. He could have been admitted to a rehabilitation institute, but her mother insisted on his receiving physical therapy at home. Ellen did not think this was right, because the quality of treatment at home was not as good as that at a facility. Her mother was strong-willed, adamant that only she could care properly for her husband. Ellen realized that her mother was being unrealistic and that caring for her father would require more time and energy than her mother could possibly provide, so she decided to quit her job or at least ask for a leave of absence in order to assist in her father's care.

The group explained to Ellen not only that she would be making an unwise move for herself, but that by complying with her mother's wishes she would be an accomplice to her father not receiving the best possible treatment. They suggested having the doctor and perhaps the minister impress upon her mother the importance of providing the best treatment available, something her home could not offer. They pointed out that if Ellen was firm in telling her mother that she would not interrupt her work for an inappropriate demand, her mother would be more apt to listen to reason. Ellen received a great deal of support from the group, and with the help of the doctor, minister, and social worker, she was able to convince her mother to allow treatment at the rehabilitation institute.

At the next session, Ellen was commended for doing the right thing. She then began to ventilate guilty feelings about her decision, since her mother was critical of the care her father was receiving, insisting that she could care better for him at home. It then emerged that Ellen had assumed the caregiving, co-dependent role all the way back to her childhood. Her self-worth was contingent on what she could do for others, and she felt that doing anything for herself was wrong and selfish. Although this was a pattern that had permeated her entire adult life, it had not become apparent until the crisis with her father. The group continued to support Ellen and urged her to see a therapist for resolution of her co-dependency. With professional help and the group's support, Ellen was able to continue her career while providing realistic and appropriate help to her parents.

Stella was a secretary for a small law firm. When the firm merged with another, she was promoted to office manager, to supervise the clerical staff and coordinate intraoffice activities. As the firm continued to grow, the demands on Stella became excessive and unreasonable, and she began to experience burnout.

Stella attended meetings of Adult Children of Alcoholics, and in a discussion meeting she presented her dilemma. She said that instead of hiring additional clerical staff, her employers were piling the work on her. She was spending many evenings and weekends at the office. When asked why she did not simply tell her employers that she was overworked, Stella admitted that it was virtually impossible for her to refuse any request. The group readily identified with Stella, since many children of alcoholic parents suffer from the "can't say no" syndrome. Self-effacement and people-pleasing are frequent characteristics of children of alcoholics.

One of the group suggested that perhaps they should practice saying no and proposed a psychodrama where one member would make a request, and each member had to refuse the request as tactfully as possible.

For example, one member said that she had to leave town for a week and asked that someone take care of her dog so that she could save the expense of a kennel. Each member had to say no politely and give a plausible reason. This was an enjoyable game, and members began to give each other scores on their tactfulness in refusal. One member could not think of any plausible reason and gave some absurd reason that provoked laughter. The group realized that this strategy had successfully defused the issue and that practice saying no within the protective confines of the group would make it easier to apply the same technique in real life.

It became apparent that Stella's difficulty in refusing an improper demand was by no means restricted to the office. She exhibited the same trait with her husband, children, and friends. Furthermore, other members of the group shared this trait with her. They therefore decided that they were going to stop their people-pleasing maneuvers and report back to the group each time they succeeded in doing so.

Eventually one of the group shrewdly observed that this change in their behavior was not all that radical. They had merely switched to pleasing the group by reporting how they were able to avoid pleasing others. The group concluded that although this was true, the strategy had yielded dividends. They were now able to refuse unreasonable requests. Stella, for example, had worked up the courage to tell her employers that she was frazzled by the workload and that they needed two more secretaries. She was pleasantly surprised that they readily implemented her suggestion. This had a ripple effect on her behavior with her family and friends, and Stella gained self-esteem and self-assertion.

The group came to realize that it had become a kind of "self." In other words, people-pleasers find it difficult to deny requests in order to please themselves, because satisfying themselves is fraught with feelings of guilt. Whereas satisfying the individual self aroused guilt, sharing the experience with the group lessened the torment of guilt. This feeling of safety within the group could eventually be transferred to an individual experience, so that they could avoid people-pleasing even in the absence of group approval. The legitimacy of refusing unreasonable requests had become internalized.

This insight and technique might have been achieved through individual therapy, but the group technique enhanced and facilitated the process. People who have attended self-help groups attest not only that they have been able to discontinue various ineffective behaviors, but also that their sense of self-esteem has significantly increased.

Part V

Understanding Self-Esteem

TWENTY-SIX

Components of Self-Esteem

Positive self-esteem is composed of competence and worth. Unwarranted feelings of incompetence can be eliminated through self-analysis and by participating in a therapeutic or self-help group. Once we discover the positive aspects of our personality, we develop much more confidence in our ability to cope with stress.

Feelings of competence and adequacy are not the only determinant of self-esteem. Suppose you had suffered a stroke, which affected your speech and walking. Are you entitled to self-esteem? If the only criterion for self-esteem is competence, then you would have no claim to self-esteem. Surely this is not so. There must be another factor. And that is worth. Human life may be thought of as having an intrinsic value apart from what we can or cannot do. This value is independent of intelligence, skills, or our contributions to society.

What is the source of this value? We can easily see how value can be based on productivity, since a productive person contributes and enriches society. If we do not consider productivity, on what basis can we consider human life per se valuable?

One major source of value for human life may be found in religious teachings. The words of Moses are an excellent example: "See I have set before you this day life and good, death and evil" (Deuteronomy 30:15). In most religions, life is equated with good, not only productive life, but life per se, whether the person is a surgeon who performs life-saving procedures or a drifter who is a social parasite. From society's perspective, the surgeon has great value and the drifter does not. From the perspective that life per se is valuable, the enormous difference between the two is insignificant. Even without a religious basis, however, human life can be considered to have an intrinsic value.

These are not philosophical concepts that are relegated to ivory-tower thinkers. These ideas can have practical application in our decision making.

For example, lives can be saved by organ transplant surgery. A person whose liver is failing and whose body is otherwise sound may have many years of life if the liver can be replaced. However, donor organs are scarce. At any one time there are a number of candidates for a liver transplant, and an available donor organ may be compatible with several potential recipients. On what basis do we decide whose life to save? Age? Marital status? Occupation? IQ? Other criteria?

Most ethicists state that there is no way of prioritizing, and organs can be allocated only on a first come, first serve basis. It is generally accepted that social value should not enter into the decision-making process. One person's life is equal to another's. There is a concept of worth that is inherent in human life. This worth is the redeeming feature of self-esteem, especially when the criteria of social value are absent. Conviction about the value of human life per se should enhance the self-esteem of the frail, the elderly, and all who realize that at any moment we may be struck by a condition that can deprive us of our functional capacity.

TWENTY-SEVEN

What Is Humanity?
What Is Spirituality?

A ssuming that there is an intrinsic value to human life, we may ask, How do we define human life?

I do not intend to discuss issues such as the irreversibly comatose patient or the patient who has suffered advanced brain deterioration, as with Alzheimer's disease. This is a category all its own. What I am discussing is the feeling of self-esteem, which does not apply to people who are in a state of global unawareness.

Science has classified humans as *Homo sapiens,* sharing membership in a group that is comprised of apes, chimpanzees, baboons, orangutans, and the like. The uniqueness that sets us apart from other hominoids is *sapiens,* or intellect.

There are many features over and above pure intellect that characterize us and distinguish us from other forms of life. We have the capacity to learn from the past, contemplate the purpose of our existence, bring about self-improvement, think about the consequences of our actions, delay gratification, and make moral choices.

All these uniquely human characteristics comprise the

spirit and distinguish humans from animals. When we exercise these capacities we are being spiritual. Note that this definition does not involve any religious orientation. An atheist will concur that humans possess these features and hence have a spirit and can be spiritual.

It follows, then, that the quality of our humanity is commensurate with our spirituality. The more we exercise our uniquely human capacities, the more excellent human beings we are. The less we exercise these characteristics, the more we approach similarity to other living things and the less we resemble the ideal human being.

A feeling of worth is within everyone's reach. People who exercise their unique human capacities to the utmost should feel very worthy as human beings, regardless of their level of education, economic status, or occupation. People who are derelict in exercising these traits, and who may feel less worthy as human beings, can gain self-esteem simply by sincerely resolving to maximize their spirituality.

The ability to maximize these human traits may vary greatly with the circumstances of one's life. If I am suffering from a severe disease, I may not be able to do much, if anything, in the way of self-improvement. But all that is necessary for a legitimate sense of worth is that I do whatever I can do at any given time.

A young woman was stricken with a particularly virulent type of multiple sclerosis. She lost her sight and then became bedridden, unable to take care of her personal needs. She required total care and could not contribute to her family in any way. This woman was nevertheless entitled to self-esteem because she accepted her suffering with faith and serenity; she was a spiritual human being. Spiritual in what way? In the acceptance of her suffering. Because it was all she could do, this was all that was expected of her.

If I have failed to maximize my spirituality, recognizing that I have been in error and resolving to correct my lifestyle is a redeeming feature. A resolve for self-improvement enhances the quality of my humanness and worth. Even serious past mistakes need not consume me with guilt or detract from my newly acquired feeling of worth.

A young woman who was working on the fourth of the twelve steps in her Alcoholics Anonymous program, making a moral inventory, had written a long list of things she had done wrong during her active addiction. I asked her whether she would now repeat such behavior, and she vehemently insisted that she would never do such things again. "If so," I said, "then all these things you have listed as negatives are learning experiences, and all learning experiences must be considered positive and listed in the positive column of the inventory ledger rather than in the negative." This is an example of the component of spirituality, learning from one's past.

Spirituality is a growth process, not a thing. Since we are always capable of self-improvement, there is never an end point to spiritual growth. The theologian Baal Shem Tov, the founder of Hasidism, was once consulted by a student who complained of severe frustration. It appeared to the student that the harder he strove to achieve a closeness to God, the more distant he was from his goal.

The teacher responded with the following example: Suppose a father wishes to teach his child how to walk. He waits until the child is capable of standing upright and then places himself very close to the child, perhaps a foot away, holds out his hands, and beckons the child to come. The child, wishing to reach the father and seeing the supportive hands so close to him, has the courage to take the first tiny step. If the father was to embrace the child at this point, the skill in walking would not be achieved. Instead, the father immediately jumps back a bit, perhaps two feet away, and again beckons to the child. The child, having successfully taken the first step and seeing the father still very near to him, ventures another step or two. Again the father retreats and continues doing so until the child learns how to walk independently.

If we were able to read the child's mind, we would undoubtedly find him frustrated. Although he continues making efforts to reach the father, it appears that the harder he tries, the more distant he is from his father. What is happening here is that there are two divergent goals. The goal of the child is to reach the father; however, the goal of the father is to teach the child how to walk independently. The father could embrace the child at any point and thereby satisfy the child's quest, but that would abort the learning

Arlo & Janis by Jimmy Johnson. Reprinted by permission of Newspaper Enterprise Association, Inc.

process. The only way the father can reach his goal is to retreat and to stimulate the child to walk.

Spirituality is a constant growth process. Once we feel we have finally achieved spirituality, we have probably lost it. If we constantly strive toward self-mastery, self-improvement, and establishing higher goals for ourselves, even sometimes with frustration, we're on the right track.

Of course, an individual can establish goals in life that do not contribute to a feeling of worth. Popping every kernel of popcorn does not get a person closer to spirituality.

A man once came to a psychiatrist's office but denied having any problems at all. "Then why have you come?" the psychiatrist asked.

"My family made me come," the man said. "They think that there is something wrong with me."

"What does your family think is wrong with you?"

"They think that I am crazy because I love pancakes."

"That's absurd. There is nothing wrong with loving pancakes. I love pancakes myself."

The man's eyes brightened. "You do! Then you must come to my home, because I have crates of them in the attic."

If I prepare several pancakes for breakfast, and perhaps a few extra to put into the freezer for later, no one will take issue with my behavior. As long as pancakes are used as food, they have a positive function. But if I accumulate so many pancakes that they no longer serve as a food item, but are assumed to have an intrinsic value, I am obviously suffering from a serious mental distortion.

We have no difficulty judging the pancake collector as mentally ill. But what about a multibillionaire who continues to work to increase his immense fortune? Money is a means for acquiring the necessities and luxuries of life. Saving money for a rainy day is equally understandable. But if I were to accumulate so much money that I could not exhaust it in many lifetimes and still continued to strive to increase my wealth, I would not appear very different from the pancake collector.

As rational human beings, and particularly as spiritual people, we should have goals that can withstand critical evaluation. There may not be universal agreement on what is a proper goal in life, but at the very least, we should be examining our lives as to whether we have goals and whether the goals are indeed appropriate.

During active drinking or drug use, people cannot see themselves as spiritual beings. In moments of clarity they may realize that they are really operating at a subhuman level, and this contributes very little to self-esteem. As sobriety progresses and they become aware of an ability to master the impulse to drink and many other destructive drives, they begin to appreciate themselves as spiritual human beings, a discovery that significantly promotes self-esteem. They become aware that whereas frustration and contentment are mutually exclusive, frustration and happiness are compatible. We can actually be happy while also being frustrated if we are aware that frustration often accompanies an active growth process. There is joy in constantly undergoing a process of self-improvement.

TWENTY-EIGHT

Helping Our Children
Develop Self-Esteem

In all my public lectures I emphasize the crucial role of self-esteem and of achieving a valid self-concept. Invariably, someone in the audience asks, "What can we do as parents to make sure our children have self-esteem?" My answer is "Self-concepts are contagious. Parents who have feelings of security and self-confidence are likely to pass these on to their children. Parents who have negative self-concepts pass those on to their children. The most effective way to instill self-esteem in one's children is for the parents to develop it themselves."

Parents who spend time with their children convey the message "You are important to me," and that is a major component of healthy self-esteem. Parents who lack self-esteem, however, avoid close relationships with their children. These parents may explain, "I have to be out there earning money to give my children what they need. If I do not put away money for their summer camp/braces/college education, I will be depriving them of a vital need." While I do not minimize the importance of these things, I must emphasize that if they are achieved at the expense of adequate parent-child relationships, the price is too high. A healthy self-esteem that comes out of a parent-child relationship exceeds even a college education.

Merely spending time with children is not enough. We must behave in ways that encourage our children's self-esteem. For example, a child must learn good from bad and right from wrong, and we must provide the necessary discipline. It is extremely important to do so in a manner that does not generate shame.

Proper parenting consists of adopting principles that promote self-esteem. Bear in mind that a child's feelings of self begin to develop in infancy, when he or she is a tiny creature living in a world populated by giants. We must remember this and try to make our children feel secure in surroundings that can overwhelm them with anxiety. Parents are the child's primary resource in a world that may appear very threatening. Bringing a child into the world carries with it an obligation of providing emotional as well as physical nurturing. Starting the child off with self-esteem is particularly crucial, because negative feelings are self-reinforcing and self-perpetuating. A child who believes that he or she will fail is likely to do so, and this failure further lowers his self-esteem, thus making the next challenge an even greater threat and minimizing chances of success.

Children need to know that they are loved, and parental love should be unconditional. Even when children misbehave, even when a grown-up son or daughter acts in such a manner that parents must sever the relationship, parental love should never disappear. I was quite young when I studied the Scriptures and read about the rebellion of Absalom against his father, King David. Absalom was merciless in pursuit of his father, yet when David ordered his generals to quell the rebellion, he instructed them to "spare the child." When David learned that Absalom had been killed in battle, he grieved for him and wept bitterly. "My son, my son. Would that I had died instead of you" (Samuel II 18:33). Parents have the capacity to love a child even when the child is a mortal enemy.

Loving a child does not mean being tolerant of the child's misbehavior. Quite the contrary. We must express our disapproval of destructive behavior in whatever way is necessary—but without making our love for the child contingent on anything. Loving parents act in the interest of the child when the child lacks the capacity to do so. A good analogy is when parents have their infant child immunized. After the first immunization the child may retain a vivid memory of the pain inflicted by the doctor in the white coat, and on subsequent visits to the doctor's office begin to cry at the sight of the white coat and even try to claw and bite the parent who restrains him. The infant may seem to hate the parent who has colluded with the doctor, but the parent nevertheless acts in the child's behalf to prevent serious diseases later in life. The same love and consideration must accompany all parental behavior that is in the child's welfare. If it is necesary to evict a grown-up son or daughter who persists in intolerable destructive behavior, it must be done with the same love that characterized restraining the child for the painful immunization.

Things that appear trivial to adults may be of great importance to children. If we dismiss these things, a child may get to feel that she is unimportant, a fundamental component of low self-esteem. When a child cries over a lost toy or a playmate who was mean, we sometimes dismiss this as "you shouldn't cry over something so silly." This is a devaluation of what is important to the child and a message that her feelings don't count.

Young children see their parents as omniscient and omnipotent. They need to be carefully weaned from this attitude. If a child thinks that his parents are infallible and that he is the only one who makes mistakes, it can depress his self-esteem. If a child learns that parents, too, can make mistakes, he is less likely to condemn himself for his errors. We should admit when we are wrong and should apologize for our mistakes. Parents who insist that a child apologize but never set an example may cause the child to consider himself the only defective person in the family.

Promises to a child should never be broken. In order for a child to develop a sense of responsibility and trustworthiness, she must have a role model for trust. There may be ways to justify "white lies" with other adults, but there is no justification for lying to children. To a child, a lie is a lie regardless of its character.

Obviously, parents must make many decisions for their children, who lack the maturity and wisdom to decide for themselves. However, whenever a child can be permitted to decide things for himself, we should encourage it. Not allowing the child to exercise his immature capacities to make decisions has the same result as not allowing him to exercise his muscles: Neither will develop. A child who is not given the opportunity to think and to act for himself may begin to think of himself as a nonentity, or as a mere appendage of his parents.

A young child accompanied her parents to a restaurant for dinner. After the waitress took the parents' orders, she turned to the child and asked her what she desired. The child responded, "Two hot dogs and a Coke." The mother smiled knowingly at the waitress and said, "You can bring her roast beef with potatoes and vegetables." Shortly afterward the waitress returned with two hot dogs and a Coke.

The mother was amazed, but the child's eyes lit up brightly and she grinned from ear to ear. "Look, Ma!" she said. "She thinks I'm real!"

From a purely scientific aspect, the mother's concept of proper nutrition was correct, but from the point of view of allowing the child to be a "self," she was in error. This is an example of how devoted, caring parents may inadvertently undermine a child's self-esteem.

Right along with acknowledging mistakes and apologizing, parents should share some of their own childhood mistakes and experiences. The goal in rearing a child is for him to become a decent and wholesome human being, not a robot or an angel. As role models, we should demonstrate that we are humans too.

Suppose my daughter gets a detention for passing notes in class. Her feelings may be a combination of humiliation, guilt, anger, and defiance. If I say, "That reminds me of when I had to stay after school and write one hundred times 'I will not pass notes in class,' and then I had to get Grandma to sign the paper," my daughter may ask, "You did? What did Grandma do to you?" "Nothing. She just said that it better never happen again, and I never did it again." Sharing this experience with a child is likely to diminish her shame and anger and actually increase her respect for authority. It allows her to identify with me and realize that when people make mistakes and learn not to repeat them, they grow up to be respectable people. Don't be surprised if the child wants to know more about the event. "Tell me again about how you were made to stay after school. Didn't Grandma scream at you? What kind of notes did you write? Did you hate the teacher?" These and similar questions indicate the child's need to vindicate herself by identifying with you. The violation of rules is not being condoned, but neither is the child being condemned.

Children need strokes and acknowledgments of their achievements. Nothing promotes trying to succeed as success. Displaying a test paper with a good grade or a child's artwork on the refrigerator door is encouraging to the child. We must look for the positives and acknowledge them.

At the same time, we should be truthful. False compliments are of no value. Children are not stupid, and if they feel that our commendation is only empty words, they will not be stimulated to receive more insincere praise.

When my seven-year-old grandson came home from his fourth violin lesson, he asked, "Do you want to hear me play?" and proudly extracted the bow from the case. Although the melody was grossly off tune, I was about to say, "That was beautiful. I'm really proud of you." I caught myself, because it was not beautiful, and to say so would have been a lie. Instead I said, "I know that tune. Let's have a concert. You play and I'll sing it." We did so, and the child beamed with pride. I had acknowledged his playing a melody that I could recognize, and I had not lied to him.

The occurrence of an emotion is neither good nor bad. Like the law of gravity, it is simply there. What we do with a particular emotion is a matter of morals and ethics and can be good or bad, but the pure emotion itself is a neutral phenomenon.

We should be keenly aware of this, because children are full of raw emotion. They must learn how to deal constructively with emotions. Improper management of emotions can be harmful, but children should not be condemned for having emotions. Children have no control over having an emotion, and condemning them for the emotion is likely to make them feel that they are bad. This is how children develop unhealthy feelings of shame.

Children may experience intense anger, hate, and envy. If we acknowledge these feelings nonjudgmentally and the child feels comfortable sharing these feelings, then even a very young child can be taught how to deal with them. But if we categorically condemn all such feelings, the child will be threatened by their exposure and will conceal them and won't have the opportunity to learn how to manage them. She may even repress them, and they will fester in her unconscious and may become the source of various personality disorders and neurotic symptoms.

Children are very sensitive. Insults or unkind words have a much greater impact on a child than on an adult. If we injure a sapling, the resulting distortion of growth is apt to be of much greater magnitude than a similar injury to a fully grown tree.

Never embarrass a child. If there were ten commandments of child rearing, this would be the first. When a child needs to be punished, do this without humiliating him in front of friends or even siblings. It's best to take him into another room where the discipline can be carried out. If he is humiliated in the presence of friends or siblings, the pain and anger at being embarrassed may turn into defiance and negate the desired effects of the discipline.

Promoting self-esteem by proper parenting is not a simple task, and there is not too much latitude for error. If our expectations are beyond the child's capacities, she may develop feelings of failure. The child won't conclude, "My parents' expectations of me are unjustified," but rather, "There must be something wrong with me that I can't do what I'm supposed to." On the other hand, if we do too much for the child and do not allow her to grow, she may develop unwarranted feelings of helplessness. Either extreme may result in feelings of inferiority, so we should thoughtfully consider our expectations, being alert and sensitive to our children's reactions to these expectations.

It is important to be as open as possible with children. Keeping secrets is fraught with dangers. First, many secrets are not well kept, and when the child discovers that something has been kept from him he may lose trust in us. He may join the charade and act as if he does not know, which ends up with everyone walking on eggs. Second, a well-kept secret may result in the child's fantasizing, and the fantasy may be much worse than the reality. That Uncle Moe was arrested for embezzlement may be very embarrassing to the family, but it is much worse if the child is allowed to fantasize why Uncle Moe no longer is at Sunday supper. The child may overhear bits and pieces about Uncle Moe, and having been exposed to all kinds of lurid tales on television, may fantasize that Uncle Moe is the serial killer or child molester who has eluded the police. Finally, a child is apt to sense that something is being concealed. When children are taken into our confidence, this enhances their esteem, whereas keeping them in the dark is apt to depress self-esteem.

Let's return to the first point in this chapter. Parents may underestimate their role as models for their children. Screaming "Stop shouting" is worthless because children will emulate the act rather than accept the verbal message. If we wallow in feelings of shame and inferiority, it will not result in our children developing a positive self-image. We can learn to grow in self-awareness and self-confidence with our children. If we avoid self-destructive behavior because it is beneath our dignity, our children will be more apt to develop similar guidelines, internalizing our behavior.

What about pushing our children to achieve? Our society is highly competitive, and there are advantages to high achievement. Should we encourage our children to achieve excellence? Are we putting them at risk of disappointment if they fail to meet that goal?

Failures are a natural part of life, not disasters. A baseball player who has a batting average of .400 can command a salary of millions of dollars a year, yet he misses hitting safely six out of ten times. Great athletes have made fumbles or struck out with the bases loaded. The prospect of failure is not a devastating threat if what is riding on it is the reality of that particular event: the ball game, the exam, the job. If a particular challenge is overemphasized, it may be invested with a greater amount of anxiety than is warranted.

Wilbur was nineteen when he came for a psychiatric consultation because he was failing in college, even though he had been a straight-A student in high school. Wilbur came from a family of coal miners. He was the first of the entire family to go to college, and his father continually boasted that his son was unique and would finally bring respectability to the family. His father took great pride in Wilbur's excellence in high school and was certain that Wilbur would perform similarly in college. He often let Wilbur know that he was gladly making many sacrifices for his college tuition and that it all was worth it because of the honor Wilbur would bring to him with his stellar academic achievement.

Wilbur reported that he studied hard and absorbed the material, but when he sat down for an exam his mind went blank. He had failed several exams, and these failures had been devastating to his self-confidence.

Far too much was riding on the exams. It was not his own academic performance that was at stake but the entire family honor and the vindication of his family's respectability. His anxiety was paralytic, causing Wilbur's mind to go blank.

But even the overemphasis on success as in Wilbur's case does not compare to the fear of loss of love. Children who feel that parental love is contingent on their successful performance are at great risk of failure.

Verbal reassurances have their limitations; nonverbal communication can be much more convincing. If children feel sincere in their parents' love for them, and that this love will not be affected by their success or failure, they are free to operate without paralyzing anxiety. It is not enough to tell children that they are loved regardless of their performance. They must feel this.

At an Al-Anon meeting, Nora narrated the ordeal of dealing with her husband's alcoholism for many years and the many blessings they enjoyed in his years of sobriety. The one major disappointment in her life had been that she could not bear a child. In her younger years she had never been denied anything she wanted, and she had great difficulty accepting her infertility. Nevertheless, they made peace with their fate and adopted two children.

Imagine her euphoria when, at age forty-two, she became pregnant. There was no question in her mind that this was direct divine intervention. This child was going to be a Rhodes scholar.

"I thought that during my years of recovery in Al-Anon all my anger and resentment had gone forever, but it suddenly returned in a massive proportion when I held my dream baby in my arms for the first time. He had Down syndrome.

" 'God, why did You do this to me? I had resigned myself to being biologically barren and adopting my two children. Why did You tease me? You are cruel and unfair.' I knew these were not nice thoughts, but I could not help them.

"Every night my husband and I prayed over the crib. 'God, You have been so kind to us. You have performed so many miracles in our lives. Now we ask You for just one more miracle. Please change him.'

"Then, after many nights of prayer, the miracle occurred. God answered our prayers, and He changed *us*.

"If that little child did not come into the world for any other purpose than what I am about to tell you, it was all worth it. When I sit in the rocking chair and cuddle him in my arms, and I look at his pudgy little hands that have only the one crease, and at his funny-looking eyes, and I realize how much I love this child with all his defects, then I know for certain that God can love me even with all my defects."

This is what is meant by unconditional love, but I am not quite sure whether Nora had the sequence of events in their proper order. She said that when she realized how much she loved the child in spite of his imperfections, then she knew that she was lovable in spite of her imperfections. I suspect it was the other way around. Nora's years of recovery in Al-Anon had brought her to a realization that she was lovable, and she had developed a healthy self-esteem. Of course it would have been a thrill to have a child who was a Rhodes scholar, but she did not need her child's performance to vindicate her. In this way, she was much different from Wilbur's father. The fact that her child would never perform brilliantly could be dealt with objectively.

Her pride and honor were not at stake, and she could love her child unconditionally.

Parental love is biological, and unconditional parental love is the natural state of a parent-child relationship. If parental love becomes conditional, it is because of the parents' low self-esteem and their need to be vindicated by their children's performance. This is why I said earlier that self-esteem is contagious and that parents who feel good about themselves are likely to pass these feelings on to their children. They can allow their children to be "selves" rather than extensions of the parents.

TWENTY-NINE

It's Never Too Late

A person may come to a self-awareness and achieve a positive self-esteem at any age. It is never too late.

During my first year of psychiatric training I was asked to see a woman in emergency consultation. The reason for the urgency never was clear to me, but I was fascinated by the story she told me in the first hour.

Isabelle was sixty-one at the time and had been abstinent from alcohol for five years. She was one of three daughters of an Episcopalian priest who enjoyed an excellent reputation in the community. Late in her adolescence, Isabelle was introduced to alcohol, and she drank alcoholically right from the start. She married at twenty, and at twenty-two had a son. When she was twenty-four her husband told her that she would have to choose between alcohol and the marriage. "I could not fool myself. I knew that I could not give up the bottle and that I was not being an adequate wife or mother. I did not contest my husband's divorce suit."

Now that she was unattached, she supported herself as an escort to some of the social elite. She was able to live quite comfortably, and there was never a dearth of alcohol.

165

After several years, the alcohol began to affect Isabelle's behavior so much that her clientele no longer desired her company. She then began catering to a lower social strata, and within a relatively short time was prostituting in a flea-bag hotel. Her family was outraged by her behavior and disowned her.

Isabelle's heavy drinking resulted in numerous hospitalizations for detoxification. Medical records of several hospitals revealed that over a twenty-two-year period she had had more than one hundred hospital admissions. Every time she was taken to Alcoholics Anonymous meetings but promptly returned to drinking after discharge.

At age fifty-six she did a strange thing. She contacted a lawyer and arranged to have the court commit her to a state mental hospital for one year. After discharge from the hospital, she obtained a job as housekeeper for a respected physician who was a widower and an alcoholic. Several times a year the doctor had to appear at governmental functions or foundation meetings, and then Isabelle would detox him and get him into respectable shape.

From a distant cousin, Isabelle learned that her son was living in New England and had two children. She wrote to her son, asking permission to visit her only living relatives, and the response was "Please stay away. We told the children you had died."

Isabelle told me all this during the first interview, and I was so fascinated by her account that I failed to ask her why she had requested a psychiatric consultation and particularly what the urgency was. As a fledgling psychiatrist, I knew that change does not occur without motivation, and there certainly had to be a very intense motivation to cause a person to place herself in a state mental hospital under court commitment for a whole year. Because of my curiosity, I suggested that Isabelle return for a subsequent appointment, and my search for the motivation continued in our weekly sessions for thirteen years. The interviews were terminated when at age seventy-four she died peacefully in her sleep.

Since Isabelle never revealed to me the secret of her motivation, which she perhaps was unaware of herself, I was left to my own devices to figure it out. My conclusion was as follows.

Every so often, a new volcano appears. Deep at the core of the earth, there is a pool of molten rock under exceedingly great pressure. Over hundreds of years, this molten lava threads its way through cracks and crevices in the earth's crust until it finally breaks through the surface and erupts. Prior to the moment of eruption, the presence of molten lava was unknown to anyone who observed Earth's surface at that spot.

I believe that at the core of every human being there is a nucleus of pride, dignity, and self-respect. Many factors may combine to conceal these feelings from one's awareness. However, like the molten lava, these feelings may slowly work their way to the surface, seeking expression. At some point in a person's life, there is a breakthrough, and the individual has at least a momentary awareness of his or her dignity and self-esteem. This realization may result in the thought, "My behavior has been beneath my dignity. I am too good a person to be acting this way." Perhaps this is what the twelve-step program refers to as a "spiritual awakening."

Occasionally when my alarm clock goes off I turn off the bell in order to sleep just a few moments more, only to wake up several hours later. Once when I had to make an early morning flight, I placed the alarm clock on the other side of the room. I knew that by the time I had walked across the room to turn it off, I would remain awake.

I believe that Isabelle's placing herself in the state mental hospital was a similar tactic. In those days there were no rehabilitation centers, and she knew no other way to avoid regressing into the behavior pattern that she now felt was beneath her dignity. This was indeed an act of desperation. Having come to a momentary realization of who she really was, she could not allow herself to be dragged into behavior that was unbecoming of her pride.

Isabelle made this radical change at age fifty-six, and the last seventeen years of her life were exemplary. She assisted countless people in recovery from alcoholism and served as a living example that "it is never too late."

THIRTY

Doing Good and Feeling Good

E veryone wants to feel good, both in terms of being free of discomforts and having positive pleasurable sensations. Some people use destructive methods to avoid discomfort and obtain pleasure—alcohol, mood-altering chemicals, compulsive gambling, eating disorders, indiscriminate sexual activity, and so on.

A common denominator to all of these destructive methods is that the sensation of relief or euphoria they provide is transient, which drives the individual to repeat the behavior in order to achieve the desired sensation.

In contrast to the ephemeral nature of destructive behaviors, the pleasurable sensation that results from having helped another human being is usually long-lasting. Thinking about a meal that I enjoyed last week may do nothing for me today, whereas the awareness that I helped someone in a difficult life situation several years ago still provides me with a sense of pride and achievement.

The experience of helping someone does not provide the momentary thrill of a drug or drink, but the durability of the good feeling more than compensates for the lack of the intense high.

One of the reasons why doing good for others can provide such a meaningful and sustained pleasurable sensation is that we identify with other people. When we help others, we attest to the value, dignity, and respectability of the person whom we consider deserving of help. This is of even greater impact when we are nondiscriminating in our will-

Peanuts® by Charles M. Schulz. Reprinted by permission of United Feature Syndicate, Inc.

ingness to help others. The message it imparts is not that a particular individual is worthy, dignified, and valuable, but that all humans are worthy, dignified, and valuable. Helping another person is thus a confirmation of our own dignity, value, and respectability. In other words, helping others enhances our self-esteem.

Not only does the benevolent act give us a feeling of pride, it also attests to our own value as caring human beings.

We have come to know Charlie Brown as having devastatingly low self-esteem. But look what happens to Charlie Brown when he has an opportunity to help another person.

Peanuts® by Charles M. Schulz. Reprinted by permission of United Feature Syndicate, Inc.

BIBLIOGRAPHY

Andrews, Louis M. *I Deserve Respect*. Minnesota: Hazelden, 1993.

Bernie, Patricia, and Louis Savary. *Building Self-Esteem in Children*. New York: Continuum, 1981.

Branden, Nathaniel. *Breaking Free*. New York: Bantam Books, 1989.

———. *The Disowned Self*. New York: Bantam Books, 1976.

———. *The Psychology of Self-Esteem*. New York: Bantam Books, 1973.

Bryant, Robert G. *Stop Improving Yourself and Start Living*. San Rafael, Calif.: New World Library, 1991.

Buxbaum, Edith. *Your Child Makes Sense*. New York: International Universities Press, 1949.

Chess, Stella. *Your Child Is a Person*. New York: Viking, 1965.

Cudney, Milton R., and Robert E. Hardy. *Self-Defeating Behaviors*. New York: Harper, 1991.

Dunbar, Flanders. *Your Preteenager's Mind and Body*. New York: Hawthorne Books, 1962.

Dunbar, Flanders. *Your Teenager's Mind and Body*. New York: Hawthorne Books, 1962.

Elkins, Dov P., ed. *Glad to Be Me*. Englewood Cliffs, N.J.: Prentice Hall, 1976.

English, O. Spurgeon. *Fathers Are Parents Too*. New York: Putnam, 1951.

Fraiberg, Selma H. *The Magic Years*. New York: Scribner, 1959.

Ginott, Haim G. *Between Parent and Child*. New York: Macmillan, 1965.

———. *Between Parent and Teenager*. New York: Macmillan, 1969.

———. *Between Teacher and Child*. New York: Macmillan, 1972.

Harris, Sydney. *The Authentic Person*. Allen, Tex.: Argus Communications, 1972.

Hegarty, Carol, and Earnie Larsen. *Believing in Myself*. New York: Prentice Hall/Parkside, 1991.

Hendricks, Gay. *Learning to Love Yourself*. New York: Simon & Schuster, 1982.

Hillman, Caroline. *Recovery of Your Self-Esteem*. New York: Simon & Schuster, 1992.

Josselyn, Irene M. *The Happy Child*. New York: Random House, 1955.

Jourard, Sidney. *The Transparent Self*. New York: Van Nostrand, 1964.

Kalellis, Peter M. *A New Self-Image*. Allen, Tex.: Argus Communications, 1982.

Larsen, Tony, *Trust Yourself*. San Luis Obispo, Calif.: Impact Publishers, 1979.

Rapoport, Rhona, Robert Rapoport, and Ziona Stelitz. *Father, Mother, and Society*. New York: Basic Books, 1977.

Robinson, Brian. *Heal Your Self-Esteem.* Delray Beach, Fla.: Health Communications, 1991.

Rogers, Carl R. *On Becoming a Person.* Boston: Houghton Mifflin, 1961.

Steincm, Gloria. *Revolution From Within.* Boston: Little, Brown, 1992.

Wheelis, Allen. *How People Change.* New York: Harper Perennial, 1976.